Captain Rob Anderson first went to sea at 15 and gained his first command of a foreign-going ship at age 29, one of the youngest captains in Australia. He has since served for 40 years as Master (Class 1, unlimited) and worked as a Great Barrier Reef and Torres Strait marine pilot, harbour Master, marine operations manager and consultant, aeroplane pilot and civil celebrant. He has also lectured part-time over ten years, proudly helping nearly 400 seafarers gain their Master 4 Certificates. His wide-ranging experience has included incidents and accidents of every type, in every ocean of the world, including twice having oil rigs sink while under tow. He lives on a small farm in country Victoria and rides high-performance motorcycles. www.captainrobanderson.com

WHEN THE SHIP HITS THE FAN

affirm
press

First published by Affirm Press in 2020
This edition published in 2023
Boon Wurrung Country
28 Thistlethwaite Street
South Melbourne VIC 3205
affirmpress.com.au

10 9 8 7 6 5 4 3 2 1

 A catalogue record for this
book is available from the
National Library of Australia

ISBN: 9781922992369 (paperback)

Cover design by Design by Committee © Affirm Press
Typeset in Minion Pro by J&M Typesetting
Proudly printed and bound in Australia by McPherson's Printing Group

WHEN THE SHIP HITS THE FAN

RIP ROARING TALES FROM A LIFE AT SEA

CAPT. ROB ANDERSON

affirm
press

CONTENTS

INTRODUCTION
MY LIFE AT SEA

My wonderful childhood in Melbourne's seaside suburbs came to a sudden end in 1965 when, at 15, I decided to go to sea. At the time, my academic career was best described as 'disastrous', so this decision was a great relief to my parents, my school, our neighbours and the local police sergeant.

I found my place in life on the deck of an old general cargo steamship trading around the Far East. The pay of £4 a week was miserable, but it seemed to accumulate alright after many weeks at sea – although any savings would quickly be blown apart over one night ashore.

It was very exciting for a kid who'd never been any further from home than Phillip Island Caravan Park, and the excitement helped to offset the frequent bouts of seasickness. By the end of 12 months, I'd discovered a profession I was good at, a lifestyle I loved and the boundless pleasures of duty-free alcohol, cigarettes and chasing girls. I had learned how to live on a ship: how to get a meal, make my bunk, keep clean and tidy, and how to do a hard day's work alongside others. I'd learned respect, too: respect for those with superior standing, but also for those with superior knowledge. I now knew how to follow orders and instructions, and also how to hand them out, and I'd learned the fundamental principle of never telling anyone to perform a task you couldn't do yourself. I'd learned that you had to earn respect, not demand it.

Eventually, I felt I'd learned as much as I could, but there was no promotion on the horizon. Though I had years of experience and some strong, well-founded skills as a seaman, it was all near worthless if I wanted to climb the rungs to become a ship's officer, a Mate, and eventually a ship's Master. For that, I would need a Certificate of Competency; I would need to go back to school.

I was lucky – very lucky. The head of the school was Captain Miller-Williams, a wonderful man, who had helped hundreds of people who were just like me: skilled in the ways of the sea, but academically dumb as dog shit. He grabbed hold of me and steered me through the minefield, and 12 very long, hard months later, I popped out the other end with a brand new Second Mate, Foreign-Going Certificate of Competency – a ticket to ride.

I surged through the next years, gaining my First Mate's Certificate and finally my Master, Foreign-Going Class 1 in record time. It's an easy path when you're doing something you love.

I was first appointed Master, of a small British-flagged ship, at age 28. I was the 'old man', as the Master is always called, but I was the youngest on the ship. From then on it was an adventurous voyage through life as a Master, and later pilot, of every size and type of ship, in all parts of the world.

A beautiful wife and daughters came along – on occasions quite literally when they travelled on the ship with me. In 1980 my new wife and I bought a small hobby farm to live on, a lifestyle that worked well with my months at sea, which were more than adequately compensated for with long leave periods at home. My girls grew to become strong, decisive and independent; one became a commercial lawyer, and the other a sub-sea installation engineer in the offshore oil industry.

For me the world was changing and technology was developing at a great rate. By the turn of the century it became very clear that some of our faithful old skills needed to be gently pushed aside and replaced with those better suited to the types of ships now being pushed upon us. Do so, or die. A Master Class 1 qualification (once valid for life) now required periodic re-validation and had to be supplemented with 20 or so other documents and compliances to remain competitive and employable. On top of that, a strange new being now reigned supreme: the OH&S and human resources manager.

Before Satcom became the norm in the 90s, the ship's Master was 'Master, under God'. When he disappeared over the horizon bound for a foreign port, months away, he answered to no one. His skill and experience alone determined whether people lived or died, and whether the owner and shareholders made money or were financially ruined. There were no committees of management and no discussions, and advice was neither welcome nor encouraged. The responsibilities of command were well established, and the Master was held in awe by lesser beings.

But when Satcom provided instant and easy communication between ship and shore, the role of the traditional ship Master was dramatically eroded. All of a sudden the mousy little man in the office paying the bills could call the shots, and the last person he wanted to deal with was some belligerent, domineering, crusty old-school ship Master!

The new breed of ship's Master needed to be compliant (cheap!) and respectful of his position on the totem pole, which was now somewhat lower than the chief accountant and human resources manager.

And to cement these new ideas, the Master was now given a large book of 'Standing Orders and Instructions', and volumes of 'Standing Operating Procedures' to follow. There was no longer any place for decision-making – 'read the book, it's all in there'. And if not, just pick up the phone and call the marine manager on the other side of the world while he's down the street ordering his almond-milk latte.

My suspicion that the world was going crazy was

confirmed when, on the final ship I was Master of, I was given a six-page guide and sign-off sheet for lighting the barbecue. By this point, one of my highly qualified bridge officers had to dedicate his working day solely to processing paper. Maybe it was time to hang up the sea-boots?

The problem was solved for me when I fell down an external ladder while my brand new, state-of-the-art ship was rolling heavily in a quartering sea. The injury to my knee and hip wasn't severe, but it was enough to preclude me from passing the annual medical because I couldn't satisfactorily perform the dreaded 'duck walk'. The 'duck walk' is just one of many medical tests. You have to crouch down with your bum on the deck and waddle around the inspector's office like a duck, which puts great pressure on your knees – try it! The test is a valid one as, thanks to numerous stairways and the constant possibility of violent motion, there is no place on a ship for anyone with weak or damaged knees.

How bizarre that after decades of ships and experience, millions of sea miles, and folders full of certificates and qualifications, I could no longer go to sea because I couldn't walk like a duck.

Duck walk or not, I'd had enough; it was time to 'swallow the anchor' and move ashore. No regrets.

Which brings me to here and now.

Sometimes the most seemingly plain and ordinary people leave me 'brought up, and all standing' – totally gobsmacked

– when they relate their journey through life. I've never really stopped and thought much about my own journey because anyone who goes to sea inevitably winds up with a few good stories. In my case, 50 years working on ships seems to have left me with a book's worth – plus a few more the publisher wasn't so keen on.

So here's a snapshot of my voyage through life.

Note:

When I first went away to sea, a ship's Master needed the following qualifications:

1. Master Foreign-Going Certificate of Competency – valid for life

When I finally left the sea as a competitive and marketable ship's Master/pilot, I held the following qualifications:

1. Ship Master, Class I, Foreign-Going, to be re-validated
2. Ship Master, Foreign-Going, Panama
3. Ship Master, Singapore MPA
4. Ship Master, Bahamas
5. Ship Master, Norwegian
6. Ship Master, Cyprus
7. Dynamic Positioning (Unlimited)
8. Pilotage Exemption Certificates: 22 ports
9. GMDS – AMSA: (Satellite Comms)
10. ECDIS – AMSA: (Electronic Charting)

11. ARPA (Automatic Radar plotting)
12. Ship Master Class 1 Advanced Medical Certificate
13. Red Cross First Aid
14. HUET (Helicopter Underwater Escape Training)
15. BOISET/TBOISET (rig safety/fire/gas)
16. AMSA Torres Strait and Great Barrier Reef Marine Pilot Licence
17. AMSA Check/Training Marine Pilots Licence
18. Bridge Resource Management: Ship Master
19. Bridge Resource Management: Pilot
20. Professional Development Program for Great Barrier Reef Pilots
21. Sea Survival/Offshore Facility
22. Ships Security Officer (DOTARS)
23. Port Security Officer (DOTARS)
24. ISM Training (Safety Management/Procedures)
25. Norwegian Maritime Administration Cert.
26. AMSA Oil Spill Management Course
27. Australian Maritime Security Card (MSIC)
28. Queensland Police: Police Certificate
29. Victoria Police: Police Check
30. Workplace Training Certificate IV

OUR LANGUAGE IS TRIED AND TESTED

'Starboard ten!'

I must have said these words 10,000 times over the 50 years I have been at sea – as a deck boy apprentice, cadet, Third Mate, Second Mate, Chief Mate, Master and pilot.

The easiest way to 'drive' a ship is by voice. If you stand at the controls and drive it yourself, pulling the levers and twiddling around with the wheel, you are locked in the one place. But if you have a man on the wheel to do this for you, you are free to roam around the wheelhouse and bridge wings and see what's actually going on. This is especially useful on a big ship, where the navigating bridge wings can extend out to a full 50 metres-plus. Same goes for the main engine controls: it's easier if you can just call out 'half ahead', 'full astern', 'stop' etc. You've just got to make sure you've got a strong, loud voice!

It takes a while to learn, and quite a while to get comfortable with, but I love it; it's second nature to me.

This approach is still used every day, even on the most

modern and sophisticated ships, and especially by port and sea pilots – of every nationality.

'Starboard ten!' and the man on the wheel will put 10 degrees of rudder onto starboard (right). He will hold that until told otherwise. 'Midships!' will bring the rudder back to zero degrees. 'Hard a starboard', 'hard a port', 'ease to five', 'meet her', 'steady as she goes', are all part of the same language. It works, and it works well.

As a kid of 15 on my first ship in 1965, a general cargo steamship on the South-East Asia trade, I was expected to do my trick on the wheel – no autopilot then. Steering a compass course was a difficult skill to master, but once learned it was very satisfying to be able to steer a ship on a straight and steady course.

The wooden wheel in this case was nearly 2 metres in diameter – bigger than me – with a nicely made Turk's head knot on the midship's spoke. The names and initials of all before me had been secretly scratched into the woodwork on the back of the wheel, out of sight of the Mates and Master.

The wooden spokes and wheel itself were loose and wobbly; a properly made ship's wheel is never glued or screwed on. It was built like a coach wheel out of loose parts and put together like a puzzle. The only thing holding it all together was the brass rim around the circumference – take the brass rim off and it would all fall onto the deck in pieces.

There's a nice feel to an old, well-used ship's wheel; it has soul.

Move on 50 years and my last ship had a joystick, linked to multiple very sophisticated systems and levels of redundancy via the computerised dynamic positioning (DP) system.

But, guess what?

Coming into a port, the port pilot will always request hand steering, and still be saying 'Starboard ten!' – same as it's always been.

As a trainee marine pilot (despite having been a Master for 20 years), it was impressed upon me time and time again to always look at the rudder indicator the instant you gave a helm order. It must, and does, become an automatic reaction.

Some crews are always getting it arse-about, going to sleep at the wheel, or just being plain stupid. Many, many, many times you ask for 'starboard ten' and look at the rudder indicator only to see nothing happen at all. 'Starboard ten, for fuck's sake,' screamed at full volume usually seems to fix things.

At times, I've asked for starboard ten and watched the rudder move to port ten. WTF!

'Oh, you mean the other starboard?' Was the reply from one Filipino helmsman.

How many fucking starboards are there?

Like all professional seafarers, I followed with interest the investigations into the grounding of the Costa Concordia in 2012. This Italian cruise ship somehow hit a rock off Isola del Giglio in Tuscany, ran aground and overturned, killing

32 people. How could an experienced and supposedly well-trained Master make such mistakes? The MCIB report is a big document and mentions that the Master chose to give the helmsman on the wheel headings to steer rather than rudder orders. Other reports suggest that the Master was not in the habit of checking the rudder indicator to ensure the helmsman was responding correctly to his order.

The distracted (ahem!) Master realised he was cutting it pretty close to the Scole Rocks and actually gave the helmsman the correct orders to cant the stern away from the rock. It is very likely that, if the ship had responded to the Master's orders, he would have got away with it. But, big mistake, he didn't look up and check the rudder indicator to ensure the helmsman was doing what he was told.

The helmsman wasn't.

The helmsman was briefly transfixed by the close proximity of the rock and the situation unfolding and did not immediately apply the rudder order given. He froze – not for long, but just long enough. By the time he woke up and applied the rudder order he'd been given by the Master, it was too late for the stern to rotate and the hull slid down the rocks with disastrous results.

If only the Master had been trained to automatically look up at the rudder indicator whenever ordering a rudder movement, the outcome may have been entirely different. It's all a lesson in the importance of knowing the terminology.

SEAFARING TERMS FOR THE LAYMAN

Able-bodied seaman (AB): a seaman able to perform all duties. A status attained by deck sailors after completing a few voyages and proving themselves.

Aft: towards the stern or rear of the ship.

Anchor clanker: informal term for an **anchor-handling supply vessel,** named after the loud noise generated when pulling the oil rig's anchor on deck.

Anchor-handling supply vessel (AHSV): a vessel engaged in oil rig operations.

Bird-dog: to investigate or pursue with great determination.

Bosun: an experienced and seasoned seaman, often regarded as tough, who answers to the Chief Mate and acts as a foreman for able-bodied seamen.

Bosun's chair: a swing-like wooden seat suspended with strong rope 'legs', used when working aloft or over the ship's side.

Bridge: the room or platform from which a ship is commanded.

Bridge officer: an officer with a station, watch or other duty that takes place on the ship's bridge.

Bulkheads: upright walls that divide the hull of a ship.

Bum-boat: a small launch that can be hired to get ashore from a ship at anchor.

Bulkies: informal term for 'bulk carrier', a type of ship.

Captain: a licensed mariner holding ultimate command and responsibility for the vessel.

CoC: Certificate of Competency. A driving licence.

Cloud-dancing: flying in, above and on top of clouds.

Coxswain: a person who steers as directed by a Mate or Master. A **Coxswain** is also called a **Helmsman**.

Dead slow ahead: an engine speed order meaning travel forwards as slowly as possible. Given when direct engine control is not available from the bridge.

Deck: the horizontal covering structure of a ship. Also used to distinguish different levels of a ship.

Deck boy: one who cleans decks and deck fittings of ships.

Deckie: a member of the deck crew of a ship. Also known as a **deck sailor**.

Deckhead: the underside of the deck of a ship.

Derrick: a basic crane arrangement for loading and unloading cargo.

Door louvres: the horizontal slates of a door that allow natural ventilation in the absence of air-conditioning. Designed to be kicked out of the door and used as an emergency exit in event of fire.

Double-bottom tank: ships are constructed with an inner and outer bottom, the space between being used to carry fuel, ballast, and fresh water.

Drilling commodities: the continuous supply of a wide range of materials required to operate offshore drilling rigs. A very expensive process.

Drillship: a merchant vessel modified for exploratory offshore drilling of new oil and gas wells.

Dynamic positioning (DP): a computer control system which automatically maintains a vessel's position and heading by using her own propellers and thrusters.

Fathom: a measure of water depth; 6 feet or 1.83 metres. A burial at sea requires a minimum of 6 fathoms, hence the phrase 'deep six'.

Flotsam, jetsam and lagan: any materials discarded to save a ship. Flotsam is swept off the deck of a ship, jetsam is purposefully jettisoned, and lagan is thrown over the ship's side to be recovered later.

Fore: towards the front of the ship.

Forecastle: the raised part of the bow, which contains storerooms for ropes, paint and equipment.

Foreign-going: any vessel other than a coastal vessel.

Full and down: a ship full of cargo and down to its load line marks, marks which indicate how submerged a ship may be while still maintaining safe buoyancy.

Fully rigged: a fully fitted-out ship. A fully rigged sailing ship.

Gangway: a raised platform or walkway providing a passage.

Gold braid: uniform jewellery, usually worn by bullshit artists and not always a guarantee that someone knows what they're talking about!

Greenie: a wall of solid green ocean water that sweeps aboard the vessel.

Hatches and holds: a hold is the area where cargo is lowered down into the ship, a hatch is the cover that goes on top of the hold.

Helicopter Underwater Escape Training (HUET): a mock-up helicopter in a swimming pool is used to instruct in how to get out of a helicopter should it crash into the sea and sink.

Indentured apprentice: an apprentice who is contractually bound to the ship's Master for a fixed period of training and care.

Integrated Rating (IR): a multi-tasked seaman with additional certification.

Lee: the opposite side to the windward side; the side sheltered from the wind.

Mast truck: the very top of a **mast**, a tall, upright post structure that carries a sail.

Master: a ship's **captain**, holding ultimate command and responsibility for the vessel.

Mate: officers, ordered by seniority (**Chief Mate, Second Mate, Third Mate**)

Medevac helicopter: a medical evacuation helicopter.

Monkey island: the deck located directly above the navigating bridge of the ship.

Motion: ships move in three axes, experiencing six motions, usually all at the same time! The six motions are pitch, roll, yaw, surge, sway, heave.

Offshore oilfields: oil and gas are always discovered in the most violent, inhospitable places such as the Bass Strait, West Africa, and the North Sea. Never in nice places like Surfers Paradise.

Offshore support vessel (OSV): specially designed ships for servicing offshore platforms and installations such as oil rigs. Colloquially known as a **rig boat**.

Pilot: a highly trained Master with navigational expertise who specialises in a particular port or area. Typically joins by launch and rope ladder, or by helicopter, to advise the Master. The Master is always in command and he can accept or refuse the pilot's advice.

Port: the left-hand side of, or direction from, a vessel. The term originates from Viking longboats which were fitted with a steering oar on the right-hand side to accommodate right-handed steering. This meant that the boat could only use the left side to go alongside a jetty in a 'port'.

Quartermaster: an able-bodied seaman assigned to bridge watch.

Reef pilot: a specialised marine pilot who navigates ships up and down the various passages inside the Barrier Reef. Usually stays onboard for two or three days.

Ringbolter: a stowaway. In the past, stowaways when caught were padlocked to a ringbolt in the deck.

Ro-ro: a roll-on/roll-off ship is a cargo ship designed to carry wheeled cargo such as cars and trucks.

Rosie: a rubbish bin.

Rudder indicator: usually fitted to the deckhead (ceiling) to indicate which angle the rudder is at.

Salvage: marine salvage is the process of recovering a ship and its cargo after sinking, being stranded ashore or any other maritime casualty.

Scupper: a drain going overside.

Sea-boots: boots without laces that can be kicked off when you fall into the sea. Lace up boots are for farmers.

Seasickness: only one known and guaranteed cure: sit under a tree.

Starboard: the right-hand side of, or direction from, a vessel. The term is derived from 'steering board'. See **Port.**

Tankie: cheap, shore-contracted labourers responsible for checking and cleaning a ship's fresh-water tanks.

Visual flight rules (VFR): a set of rules for pilots to follow when operating an aircraft in clear conditions.

Weather deck: a ship's deck with no overhead protection; the uppermost deck.

Wharf, jetty, pier, quay: wharfs and piers are built on piles, jetties and quays are built on fill.

Wharfie: a person who works at a wharf; a waterside worker or labourer.

Zip-line: a taut wire, sometimes called a flying fox.

MY OLD MAN

When my dad stepped off the gangway at the end of a career in the British Merchant Navy during the Second World War – after being bombed, torpedoed twice and left adrift in a lifeboat for six weeks – he was damaged in ways they didn't even have words for back then. Like many men who had been through similar experiences, he used alcohol as a way of escaping his demons and the reality of life. These are things I can understand and even sympathise with now, but when I was a kid I couldn't see past the terror of living with him, a bully of the highest order.

Not long after the war, while in port in the UK, he went to an ice rink to watch a show. My mother was one of the professional ice skaters in the troupe (her father had owned several ice and roller rinks around Great Britain). I'm not sure how it all happened from there except that they were married pretty quickly. This type of spur-of-the-moment behaviour was common back then because people struggled to imagine a future after the war and no one was sure it wouldn't flash off again at short notice, so they grabbed happiness where they could.

The war ended in 1945, they were married in 1947, I was born in 1949 and we left for Australia in 1950. My father had been to Australia many times before and during the war, and must have sold the idea to my mum. It would have looked like an attractive option compared to the exceedingly grim post-war Britain.

Dad came out to Australia on the big, fast cargo ship he was working on (Federal Lines' *Durham*), but Mum and I came out as immigrants on the *Georgic*, a White Star Line ship that had been bombed and partially sunk in Suez during the war, then salvaged and hastily refitted as a troop carrier before eventually being switched back to a passenger ship.

When he came ashore in Melbourne after a long, exciting, dangerous career at sea, my dad had very little chance of having any sort of 'normal' life. He was intelligent and well educated, at times kind and caring, but mostly very tough and demanding. He'd been born in Assam, India, to elderly parents and then sent off to an English boarding school at a very early age, and then went to sea. He had never experienced a normal family life at all. He was prone to periods of extreme anger, especially when drunk, and my two little sisters and I would hide with our mother in a bedroom while he systematically smashed up our house. Sometimes she would bundle us up and we would flee to a friend or neighbour's place to escape his fury. Those days were very scary, and I remember them vividly.

Dad worked ashore as a cargo superintendent when the industry was booming, cargo ships coming and going in huge numbers to try to get the world back on its feet. He was a tough guy in a very tough environment. With the notorious Waterside Workers' Federation on the scene the waterfront was a very dangerous place, populated by very dangerous people, and my dad had to deal with them daily. As kids we were never allowed to answer the phone because of the regular threats he received from anonymous callers.

Dad persevered with his job as a cargo superintendent, but this work was well below his capabilities and experience, and he eventually moved into marine salvage, where he made a name for himself as a very competent and professional Salvage Master. As he climbed higher, he started to leave the family behind and things got even worse at home. It was exciting when he returned from some exotic place and we'd all dress up for his homecoming, but I realise now that this sort of love and attention must have been alienating and discomforting for him. After he was back for a couple of days, the drinking would start and the rage would take over.

My mother never drank alcohol and, naturally, grew to despise it. Instead, she discovered – and grew increasingly dependent upon – the escape provided by sedative drugs such as valium. She spent much of her time totally spaced out and became an addict in the true sense of the word.

We, and I, became progressively more scared of my father. I still remained immensely proud of him, despite his fits of rage and anger, and wanted nothing more than his praise – but this, unfortunately was never forthcoming. It became a great relief to us all, and me in particular, each time he went away for work.

When I decided to go to sea myself, my dad furiously objected. He'd sent me to a fine school in the hope that I could become a professional of some kind – maybe a lawyer or doctor, who knows? More simply, I think he really wanted me to become someone better than himself. I had no interest in anything like that and school was miserable for me. The more I discovered about the sea, the more determined I became to follow that path. I waited until my mum was zonked on valium (I didn't have to wait too long, to be fair) and got her to sign my papers and passport application. The minimum age was actually 16, but I was just a few months shy and managed to slip in the door. I had to get out.

GOING TO SEA

Before I joined my first ship, I had never been more than 20 miles from my family home – although I had managed to get into a lot of trouble within that narrow radius. I hated my school: I had no time for singing hymns, acting in plays, wearing a strict uniform or being bullied by old bastard teachers. I did everything I could to be disruptive, rude and brutal, and soon started to mix with a wild crowd. Things hit their peak when, after being caned by the vice principal, I lead a group of friends into stealing his magnificent Humber Snipe and driving it off the boat ramp at Sandringham.

Though Dad had always forbid me to go to sea, in light of my recent, wayward behaviour he realised it might actually be a good option. If not for me, then definitely for him!

So at 8am on 26 January 1965, at 32 South Wharf, I joined a British Flag general cargo ship bound for Yokkaichi, Japan. An apprenticeship was the usual way to start a career at sea, but since the minimum age to be an apprentice was 16 and I was still 15, I 'signed on' as a deck boy. Then when I turned 16 I signed on as an 'Indentured Apprentice to the Master'.

My dad left me at the foot of the gangway with my bag and a new haircut, and then with a cheerful (thankful?) wave he promptly fucked off.

The five-hatch ship was working cargo and it took some fancy footwork to dodge the bales of wool being loaded by the wharfies. I crawled up the wooden gangway and was met by a Chinese Quartermaster, who eventually managed to direct me to the Chief Mate's office. When I knocked on the door, a very tall and immaculately uniformed Mate came to the doorway, inspected me like I was some kind of insect, said 'Hmmmmm', and then disappeared back inside and slammed his door shut.

I waited, and waited, and eventually a scruffy fat kid in very dirty work clothes came along. He eyed me from a distance, casually picking his nose, and appeared to decide his nasal contents were of far more interest than me.

'There,' he said eventually, pointing with a dirty fingernail, then fucked off.

I dragged my bag in the direction he'd pointed and went into a large cabin fitted with four bunks and a washbasin. Three of the bunks seemed to be in use, but one lower bunk looked free, with just a bedspread and a few girlie magazines strewn around. So I threw my bag on the bunk and sat down.

After some time the door burst open, and in came the dirty kid along with two more shifty-looking sorts.

'What the fuck do you think you're doing?' yelled the fat kid, throwing my bag across the cabin. 'That's mine, and that's

24

my bunk on top,' he yelled, 'and the other two are taken, too! You're the new apprentice, so you don't get a bunk. You can sleep on the desk next door. Fuck off.'

I went next door, a little cabin used for study, put my bag down and sat in a chair. After an hour or so, the fat kid and the two other apprentices burst in and told me to put my 'shit gear' on and get to work.

I opened my bag and my new work shirts, pants and boots fell out on the deck.

'I'll have them,' said fatso, and helped himself. He went next door, gathered up his old, dirty worn-out clothes and dropped them at my feet. 'There ya go, that'll do ya,' he said.

The clothes stank and didn't fit, but I put them on and followed the three amigos out onto the deck. I was given a paintbrush and a tin of stone-coloured paint. We painted every fucking thing on that ship! Funnels and mast tops, down to cargo holds and bilges. As the cheapest labour onboard we were given the shitty jobs. It was meant to be a period of training and education, but all ships treated the apprentices the same way: cheap labour.

At the start, *everything* seemed to be a problem, and it took me days to figure out how and when to work, how and when to get something to eat, and how to find my way around. No one spoke to me; there was not a kind word or gesture from anyone. I made up a bed under the desk, and lived out of my bag. The other two apprentices seemed to be at the beck and call of fatso, and seemed to be under strict instructions not to help me in any way.

After five days, the loading was completed and the ship was made ready to sail. There seemed to be a lot to do and it was interesting to see. As I got a little more confident with what I was doing on deck, I also got more pissed off with fatso and his ways; a showdown was inevitable. One afternoon as we crossed paths in a passageway, he pushed me out of the way; and that was it.

I belted him in the face, then landed a couple more blows for emphasis. While he was down on the ground, I kicked him in the balls and anywhere else I could find. The other two stood there aghast, mouths flapping open, and I made it clear I was ready to give them a taste, too. I'd had enough.

I went back to the cabin – the halfdeck as I'd learned that it's known as – and threw fatso's belongings off the bunk he'd been using as a sofa. I found my new clothes and boots, and kicked his shitty old clothes across the deck. No one said a word – there was nothing to say, really.

From that moment on, everything changed. The Third Mate, not long out of his apprenticeship himself, gave me a pat on the shoulder as he passed by in the afternoon. 'Good work,' he said, and gave me a reassuring smile. Then I noticed others: engineers, deck crew, stewards and cooks all seemed to be a little bit more friendly and helpful.

By the time the ship sailed, I was okay. I had a bunk, some friends, and an appetite for adventure. But I had no idea how crazy it could be.

WHAT A START ...

My very first voyage.

I'd barely left Melbourne before, and here I was on a cargo ship heading to Yokohama. Everything was awkward, difficult, and hard to understand coming straight from a suburban home. Little did I know that this was to become my life.

The British Flag general cargo ship I was on was a steamship with officers who were British or Australian, and a crew who were Chinese, which was a common combination in those days. The officers lived in grand style in the main accommodation, and most of the crew lived down aft in the poop, in a rabbit warren of cabins and passageways that included their own galley and washrooms. The exceptions were the officers' stewards, along with the cooks, butcher, laundryman, baker etc., who lived deep down in the main accommodation so they could be at the beck and call of the Master and his officers. Us four deck boys were in our tiny bunk room on the halfdeck with no TV, no internet, no air-conditioning; just fans and steam heaters.

That was the way it was, and everybody was happy with it.

There was little in the way of entertainment on ships at sea in those days; out of necessity many of us learned to enjoy reading, but for the Chinese crew it was all about gambling – and specifically mahjong. Sometimes the stakes would get pretty high – it was not uncommon to hear that someone had lost a month's wages in one hit.

A week out of Japan, heading north and approaching the Marianas, we were trying to sleep through a still, humid night. Suddenly a blood-curdling scream came from outside the halfdeck. All four of us deck boys ran outside in our shorts and bare feet, following the screams down to the poop deck. We stopped at the ladder-head and peered down. At the bottom we saw one Chinese steward covered in blood from head to foot, and another one, equally bloodied, swinging a meat cleaver.

Spotting us, the man with the cleaver made a dive for the stairs. We ran inside and down one of the long passageways. Heads peered out of each doorway as we screamed past, but soon ducked in when they saw what was coming. As the man started to gain on us, I picked up a big, heavy wooden box full of sand (for cigarette butts) and threw it at him, which just made him angrier, and more focused on us!

We ran up the stairs and pulled the door of our cabin closed behind us, holding on to the handle with all our might. The madman smashed in the louvered kick panel at the bottom of the door and swung the bloodied cleaver at our bare feet. We were slipping and sliding from the blood we'd picked up on our feet in our frantic dash. There seemed to be blood everywhere, and lots of screaming and yelling in a variety of languages.

I realised that he must have been crouching down to hack at us through the small opening at the base of the door, so we gave the door a mighty heave open and knocked him on his arse. Taking our chance, two of us jumped and lay on the madman; several engineers joined in the fray, and he was finally subdued.

I grabbed the cleaver, now covered in sticky blood and matted hair, from his hand and ran to the head of the stairs. I don't know what I intended to do, but when I looked down the stairwell there were a lot a scared, angry faces looking back up at me. I realised that some of them must have thought it was me doing the damage, so I threw the cleaver down the stairs and ran away. I was 15 years old.

The madman was handcuffed and chained to a bunk in a spare cabin, while us deck boys helped the Master tend to the wounded. We looked after a kindly Chinese steward named Wong Fat who had several deep gashes across his ear and face, until the Mate took over.

It turned out the madman had been on a mahjong losing streak. It got to the point where he'd lost the equivalent of a year's wages and just snapped.

Eventually we got ourselves and the ship cleaned down, and took turns keeping watch over the madman. The ship's electrician jury rigged a switch and bell to the bridge – if he got loose we were to throw the switch and run like fuck!

One man was very severely injured, so the Master decided to divert to the island of Guam, then a big US base for the B52 bombers going to Vietnam. It was quite exciting to go into the port and see the ships and planes. We were able to get the wounded man to the hospital, but the authorities wouldn't take responsibility for the crazy guy, so he had to remain onboard.

As we continued to Yokohama, I was on watch at the doorway to the cabin where the madman was chained up. He was pretty subdued, and hadn't really caused us any concern since we'd managed to lock him up – but you never knew. When I looked out onto the weather deck, I spotted around half a dozen of the Chinese deck crew standing there quietly, each holding a heavy steel hatch bar. The Chinese Bosun stepped into the light. He was a huge man from Hainan with a strong round face, and he had always been very kind and caring to us boys. We all had a great respect for him: he was the ultimate seaman and a Master of his trade.

'Number Four,' he said. He always called us by our seniority number; I was number four deck boy. 'Please go away for a small time and leave us to fix this problem.'

The men were deeply upset that such a thing had happened onboard and felt that they should fix the problem themselves. I guessed that this 'fix' wouldn't end well for the madman. (More than likely straight over the side …)

'Bosun, I can't,' I mumbled, discreetly pushing the switch.

I wasn't scared, because I knew that the Bosun would never hurt me, nor ever let anyone else hurt me, but I could see the determination in the men's eyes. To my great relief, the Chief Mate arrived and calmly spoke the Bosun down. It was a valuable lesson to me, at a very early age, on how to command people with respect. The madman made it ashore. He was arrested in Yokohama, sent back to Hong Kong and gaoled, never to be seen again.

Many years later, I was Second Mate on a beautiful passenger cargo ship when a new batch of Chinese crew joined us in Hong Kong. In those days the Mates had our own steward to look after us – he would clean our cabins, make our bunks and lay out our uniforms for the day. (What a life!) Imagine my surprise when the new steward turned out to be Wong Fat, the man who had suffered those terrible slashes across his face, and who my friends and I had helped as deck boys. Meeting again after all that time was a very emotional moment for both of us, and although it wasn't accepted practice amongst seamen in those days (or these, come to think of it), we embraced as old friends.

Wong Fat carried four deep scars across his cheeks and ear from the meat cleaver, which meant that he wasn't put to work on the passenger decks, but he was very happy to look after us, and me in particular. We had a strong bond while we sailed together, and I remember him fondly as I write this now.

RUNNING OF THE BULLS

Part of the reason I decided to go to sea was that I couldn't stand the thought of working on a farm: the smell of shit, flies, dirt, dust and the smell of more shit. Dad had sent me away to a farm for a few school holidays and I'd hated it, and everything about it. I wanted to get as far from that kind of work as I could.

Unfortunately, there was no escaping the dreaded farm animals. My next interaction with livestock came on one of my first voyages as a deck boy. We'd discharged general cargo at Pyrmont and found ourselves shifted around by tugs to Woolloomooloo, where we went ashore to the pub across the road and then up the hill to King's Cross. Giddy up! The next day arrived much too quickly, and it wasn't good: our next job was a full-deck cargo of livestock bound for the Philippines.

Keep in mind, that ship was the epitome of an everyday cargo ship of the 1960s: five hatches with union purchase derricks, steam turbines and definitely no air-conditioning. A gang of wharfies and a heap of riggers trooped onto the foredeck and afterdeck to construct pens from scaffolding pipes and fittings. Then load after load of hay and fodder was piled on top of the hatches and tarped down. There were individual, stand-up-only pens for a hundred beasts that were roofed off with marine ply and had water troughs fitted. *What about the shit?* I wondered as I watched the structures going up.

After a week of this hectic activity, I wandered out on deck one morning to find row after row of cattle trucks parked up and down the wharf and out onto the Woolloomooloo roadway. The trucks were jammed tight with cattle, mainly huge Brahman bulls.

As the sun rose, so did the smell of shit and piss – I was worried, very worried, and they weren't even on the ship yet. Big, heavy gangway runs were lifted up from the wharf onto the ship, and rolls of hessian were rigged to make a 'run' for the animals to follow around the various deck obstacles, such as winches, ladders and hatchways. There were even stockmen there to run the beasts from the trucks, up the gangways and along the slippery steel decks to the pens. Real fucking cowboys!

In a very short time the decks were awash with shit and piss, and I was literally in the thick of it, having been instructed by the Mate to 'lend a hand'. I had never in my life seen such big animals: a Brahman bull is an impressive sight from the front, but it's even more impressive from astern, where its huge balls swing free. These were breeding bulls bound for the Dole Pineapple Corp farms in the Philippines, where they would be fed the very rich waste products of the pineapple processing farms and factories.

It took several days to get the animals onboard and locked down in their pens, and they soon made it clear that they weren't happy, bellowing and moaning throughout the night.

Our cabin was on the weather deck (main deck) in the waist of the ship, the lowest point before the ship's deck curves upwards towards the bow and the stern. This meant that all of the piss and shit flowed down the decks to a point right outside our cabin window. Since there was no air-conditioning, that window was usually open.

As the liquid shit blocked the scupper drains, the waist filled up and up with shitty piss until it reached the freeing ports, so there was always a foot of bovine sewerage slopping around to greet us as we stepped outside our cabin every morning. The stench was horrible, especially to our delicate sailorman nostrils. Eventually we sailed our way up Sydney Harbour, leaving a long streak of cow shit in our wake.

We set off for a small port called Dadiangas on the island of Negros, about three weeks away via the Great Barrier Reef inner route and Torres Strait. There were two cowboys onboard and the three of us deck boys were assigned to be their assistants – just my fucking luck!

Every morning we turned-to at 5.30am and struggled into our 'shit gear': boots, shorts and a belt with a knife and marlin spike. No hat, no shirt, no sunscreen – these were very different times. The boots soon filled up, so it was down to bare feet in a flash. First job in the morning was to rig the fire hoses and wash down the night mess. Each hose needed two of us to handle it, and the third kid did his best to help with a deck broom and a rod to poke the scuppers clear of the cow-shit soup.

As we steamed towards the Philippines, we hit a fierce tropical depression – not a cyclone, but not far from it. The ship pitched, rolled and heaved, and the job was twice as hard and ten times more dangerous. The animals were becoming restless, bad tempered and no doubt scared by the violent motion of the ship and occasional waves crashing on deck. We faced the very real risk of being washed along the walkways and under the feet of the bulls, which, we were warned, would likely kick, bite and jump on us at the first opportunity.

At about 3am one morning we were called out; a greenie had swept the deck and carried away a large section of the pens on the port side of the foredeck. About 20 of the 100 animals onboard had been swept overboard into the dark, rough sea, and another ten or so were down and struggling.

The ship was hove-to, head to weather, and all hands were turned out to help. But the Chinese deck crew had no idea, and no intention of doing much. We were very scared of the bulls; they were fucking terrified! We worked all through the night with the cowboys using blocks and tackles and cargo winches to sort the mess out and get the surviving animals back on their feet.

As is always the case, by the time morning came the weather had moderated quickly. The sun came out and, just like nothing had ever happened, the normal routine resumed. At long last we arrived at Dadiangas and a local pilot took our ship up a very narrow and poorly marked waterway to a wharf that seemed to stick straight out of the jungle. We ran the ship's mooring lines ashore where the Filipino workers made them fast to palm trees and a large gangway was rigged.

While running out one of our long and expensive mooring ropes, the man on the beach kept signalling for *more slack, more slack!* Our rope kept disappearing over the side and into the jungle, until we had only the bare minimum onboard to turn up on the drum end. After a long delay and fuck all happening, the Third Mate gave the order to heave it in … but there was nothing left to heave with. They'd dragged the mooring rope into the jungle, cut it, and fucked off. The captain was apoplectic.

The hessian blinds were tied up and everything prepared for an early-morning start. We were all excited to be rid of our stinking cargo so we could clean down our ship and get back to normal. At 5am we met up with the cowboys, who told us that we would have to 'tail' each bull out of his pen and then 'steer' him down the hessian run to the gangway – WTF?!

What that meant was, we would have to hang onto the animal's shitty tail, and when it took off, we'd have to twist and bend the tail to direct the bull. One of the cowboys said he'd do the first few and show us the way. When he yelled out, I slid the bar away and was nearly knocked flat as a tonne of bull took off with the cowboy in close pursuit, twisting and pulling the tail to send him in the right direction. The huge bull took off down the deck, glad to be free at last, its hooves slipping and sliding on the painted steel deck. It roared down the gangway like a locomotive, much to the surprise of the new Filipino 'cowboys' who were standing onshore. They'd obviously never seen anything like it in their lives, but the bull was their problem now.

'Okay, you do the next one!' our cowboy said to me, and I crawled around the back of the pen and grabbed hold of the next bull's tail.

'Let her rip,' I yelled, and the bull went from zero to maximum in two paces. My feet never touched the deck. All I could see were a massive set of balls flogging around, ready to smack me in the face, and some thrashing, skidding hooves. At the third pace, the bull expelled a mighty blast of liquid shit that covered me from head to toe.

Squinting through the shit, I somehow remembered to steer the animal around the obstacle course of winches, hatches and ventilators across the shit-wet, steel deck. The bull didn't give a fuck where it was going; it just wanted to get out of that pen as fast as possible. I held on for grim death and went for the ride. By the time I had the wherewithal to let go, I'd already gone down the gangway and was halfway up the wharf and on the road to town. As I tumbled in a dusty ball on the ground, I was nearly run over by a Jeep full of Filipino cowboys in hot pursuit of the runaway bull.

I limped back to the ship, found my hat, and headed up the gangway covered in shit and dust. Suddenly I had to jump aside to avoid being trampled by the next bull making its break for freedom. As it shot past, I got a flash of another wide-eyed, shit-covered deckhand hanging on to its tail.

'Not bad,' said the cowboy when I'd made it back on deck. 'Only another 95 to go.'

A DANGEROUS JOB

Merchant ships are constructed in such a way that allows the spaces between frames and double bottoms to be used to store fuel, salt-water ballast and fresh water. These are very confined spaces, only accessible by heavily bolted manholes. The fresh-water tanks are cement-washed to provide clean surfaces for the ship's supply of fresh water, and they need to be regularly checked, cleaned and resurfaced. This was always a bastard of a job, and usually left to cheap, shore-contract labourers ('tankies') in countries such as Hong Kong and India.

The tanks were very low, dark, damp and dingy, and the workers could spend days in there scraping, cleaning then applying the cement wash with big brushes. On completion, the tank had to be inspected by an officer (a task to avoid) to ensure the work had been done satisfactorily; all tools, rags and equipment had been removed; and that all the workers had left. Then the ship's engineers would bolt down the manhole cover using a rubber seal and 40-odd bolts. The tank was then filled with fresh water and pumped out a few times to get rid of the surplus cement wash before it was signed off as ready for use. Theoretically.

Sometimes the officer would just stick his head in the manhole, flash his torch around and declare the tank clear and ready for 'boxing up'. The ship would then load cargo, usually over the top of the manhole cover, and head off to sea.

A week or so into one voyage in the late 60s, some of the officers and crew began to complain that the water was 'off'. The experienced Chief Mate twigged that something was up and had the engineers switch to another tank. Many weeks later, after the cargo had been unloaded and the manhole cover unbolted, the ghastly smell and oily muck proved pretty conclusively that the tank had *not* been inspected, and that a tankie had been sealed inside. A nightmare that doesn't bare thinking about (or describing).

Years later I delivered a few ships to Gadani beach in India for scrapping. There, huge ships of every type and size are run ashore on the shelving beach, then an army of workmen progressively chop it up for scrap. It is a nightmare of a place, in every respect – life is cheap, and accidents are plentiful.

As the ships are progressively dismantled, the tanks – fuel, ballast, fresh water – are fully exposed for the very first time since the ship was built. And sometimes the contents of these tanks are very disturbing. On my first arrival at Gadani beach, I went ashore to the foreman's office to await a taxi and was startled to see a wide range of bones laid out along his office wall. They were all worn down and rounded from years of rolling around in a tank. And there were lots of them.

A SNAG IN THE SHACKLE

There was a time when we had quite a fleet of passenger ships moving around the Australian ports. Before affordable air travel it was a pretty good option when going to places not easily serviced by trains.

On one such ship, travelling down the East Coast of Australia in fair weather, the Mate was doing his afternoon rounds with the Bosun. As they stepped out the door onto the passengers' open promenade deck, they were surprised to see a large group of passengers all gazing skywards.

On looking up they saw one of the ABs (able seamen) in a Bosun's chair (a sort of wooden swing seat used when working aloft), which had a running shackle around one of the mast stays to keep him close to the wire. On a good day it was an easy job, and obviously kept the passengers amused, too – although this group seemed particularly animated.

WTF! Suddenly the Mate realised why: the end of the AB's very substantial cock was hanging out the leg of his shorts! The Mate yelled at the Bosun to get that fucking man down. The Bosun started yelling at the AB, who peered down at them, but he was so far up the mast that he couldn't hear. Soon both the Bosun and the Mate were attempting a weird sort of charade, trying to explain what the problem was.

The message finally got through, and the AB looked down and waved back that he understood. Being a good sailor, he had a knife and spike on his belt. He stretched out the big white cock, neatly cut it off and threw it in the drink. Several people fainted, including the Mate. Amazing what you can do with a pork sausage from the galley.

A SURPRISE CATCH

Hong Kong was a regular port of call for general cargo ships. Sometimes we'd come down from Japan via the China Straits, and sometimes we'd come up from Manila or Singapore in the South. The traffic would build up as we got closer to Hong Kong, with many small fishing vessels – usually sailing junks from mainland China – getting in the way.

When approaching Hong Kong – and only Hong Kong – we were always told to go forward and check the anchors. No one ever told me why, or what the fuck I was looking for; it was just the done thing in Hong Kong.

The penny didn't drop until many years later, when I was sitting in a nice coffee shop at the Ocean Terminal admiring a beautiful, state-of-the-art Swedish cargo ship making its way up the harbour. But something wasn't quite right – hanging off the anchors were the sails, mast and rigging of a sailing fishing junk! Obviously, the cargo ship had run the junk down overnight, and no one had gone forward to check.

Finally it all made sense!

BRANDING HORSES

With general cargo ships, you never knew what to expect or what load you'd be carrying, which was generally repetitious, except when it wasn't. Carrying 100 horses from Sydney to the Philippines was one of those trips that wasn't.

A gang of shore contractors came onboard and, using scaffolding pipe and clamps, made up the standing-room-only. The horses, which I believe were polo ponies or breeding horses, came onboard up a long gangway, and horsemen coaxed and steered them into their pens. We deck boys loaded up their feed drums, hay nets and water tubs as directed by the horsemen.

Off we went, up the coast, up the inside of the Barrier Reef, and on to the little port of Dadiangas in the Philippines. We settled down into a routine: wash down all the shit and piss with a fire hose in the morning, dole out the feed, fill the water troughs. None of us liked the smell, and we all sported bite marks from the increasingly bad-tempered horses, but so far, so good. That was until the radio operator received a message (by Morse code in those days) that someone had fucked up and forgot to brand the horses before they were loaded. We wouldn't be permitted to unload the horses in the Philippines unless they were branded with the letters 'IMP' for 'imported'.

First of all, where do you get a brand in the middle of the Coral Sea?! We had ten engineers onboard and, as is always the case, they were hands-on, resourceful types who had completed their apprenticeships in huge workshops and engineering works. So they carved a beautiful 'IMP' out of a piece of angle iron, adding on a nicely turned wooden handle to protect our delicate little fingers. It was a work of art … except they'd forgotten to reverse the lettering.

So they banged up another one, nowhere near as flash but at least the right way around this time. The 44-gallon drum we occasionally used as a barbecue was perfect to heat the branding iron, but there was still one more problem to overcome: how the fuck do you brand a horse?

So the Master got the radio operator to bang and clatter away for days on his Morse key trying to get technical details on how to brand a horse. He used a speed key: pushed to one side it sent continuous 'dits'; pushed the other side it sent continuous 'dahs'. The word 'horse' for example was: 'dit dit dit dit, dah dah dah, dit dah dit, dit dit dit, dit'. At sea in the 60s this was as close as you could get to Googling something. Eventually the radio operator managed to get down pages and pages of information on how to brand horses.

The Master, being a very competent and experienced seaman, promptly handballed the whole mess to the Chief Mate – 'Fix it!'

The Chief Mate took one look and passed it to the senior apprentice – 'Get it done!' WTF!

The apprentices all gathered around the instructions and tried to make sense of them. The most mysterious part of 'The Idiot's Guide to Branding a Horse' was the repeated reference to a 'twitch'. What the fuck was a twitch? Where would we find one? Where did it go, and what was it for? Much later in life, with a horsey wife and daughters, I learned that a twitch is a stick with a piece of cord on the end that you twist around the horse's upper lip. (Sailors call this kind of device a 'Spanish windlass' – if someone had told us that we would have known immediately.) Apparently, a horse's roped-up lip is quite sensitive to movement (no shit) and so they can be held nice and steady while you hit them with the brand. It sounds easy now, but to dumb-arse deck boys who'd barely even *seen* a horse, the pages and pages of directions were impenetrable.

Still, somehow we sorted it out and the big day arrived. The Master and all the officers stood on the boat deck to watch the performance. With the first horse twitched up, we drew a circle on his shoulder with chalk and got the brand glowing red in the charcoal fire. Too easy. When all was ready, I pulled the brand out of the fire and … there was nothing on the end. The letters had fallen off. In their rush to make the second brand, the engineers had welded some of the letters and they had cracked off in the heat. Back to the drawing board, off with the twitch, and the Master and Mates retired for pre-lunch G&Ts.

The next day, new brand in hand, we got going again and, to the disappointment of the gallery, got into our stride branding the horses. It all went off without a hitch, with lots of smoke and the smell of burning hide. That's when the engineers found a use for their first, finely crafted branding iron. They grabbed the youngest deck boy, put him on the hatch face-down and pulled down his shorts, his little pink bum skywards. Then they pulled from the coals the red hot brand we'd been using and branded a piece of meat right under his nose, where he could see the meat burning and smell the smoke.

He was screaming!

Unbeknownst to him, though, the first brand was put in a bucket of ice, out of his sight. At the last minute, it was substituted and banged on the cheek of his arse. He let out a mighty scream and passed out.

Everybody thought it was a great joke and headed off for a beer, and our deck boy came good, pulled up his shorts and made a run for it.

But, it turned out ice was not that much kinder than fire. Without realising, they had effectively 'freeze-branded' the boy, and so he had the reversed letters 'IMP' imprinted on his bum for the rest of his life.

It was a different world then. Nowadays he'd be off to see a lawyer.

1 PAT PONG ROAD

We had delivered a passenger cargo ship from Hong Kong to Taiwan, and run it up on the beach there for scrap. The six of us had a ticket home, but we were young men in the late 60s so cashed in our ticket and headed to Bangkok for some fun and adventure.

We eventually found ourselves at the corner of Pat Pong Road, outside No. 1. This street went for miles and was door-to-door bars of illicit repute – just what we were looking for. One of the engineers had been before and knew how it worked. Standing in the burning hot sun, on the corner, he suggested that as it was early in the day we should move from bar to bar up and down each side of Pat Pong Road, have a beer or two, and then head back and settle for the long term in a bar we all liked. Great plan. That's why he was an engineer!

Into No. 1 Pat Pong Road we charged, and didn't come out for three days. Never even saw No. 2 Pat Pong Road.

SIR JOHN'S FAGS

Prior to going for my Second Mate's Certificate, I worked on a salvage ship as a sort of deck boy shit-kicker. The owner and operator of United Salvage was Captain Sir John Protheroe Williams, a giant in the shipping industry and a legend in marine salvage. It was he who recovered the gold bullion from the deepwater wreck of the Niagara, well documented in his book *Gold from the Sea*.

A slightly built Welshman with a fierce look in his eye, Sir John was very scary to the likes of me, the lowest form of marine growth. Back in the 1920s he had become Bosun on a four-masted fully rigged ship at the age of just 25 – which was quite some achievement. By the time I met him he was a self-made multi-millionaire. But he had one weakness, and that was smoking. He smoked continuously, and it was obviously affecting his health.

One day, Sir John came out in the tug to pay us a visit and see how the job was progressing. The removal of the wreck of the inter-island ferry *Wahine* was progressing – but slowly. Out of respect, the tug and the salvage ship both flew Sir

John's own (registered) flag: it featured the Welsh green-and-white cross, but in place of the Welsh dragon was a seahorse with a gold bar in its mouth.

Sir John bounced aboard and was met by the salvage Master and all the big dicks; I was lurking around in the background in my dirty work clothes and boots, but Sir John's reptilian eye found me.

'Come here, boyo – take these, and when I ask for them, don't give them to me,' he said, handing me his cigarettes before trotting off to inspect the job. I tagged along behind the pack of arse-creepers. After about 15 minutes, Sir John stared patting down his pockets. He swivelled around and focused on me.

'Give me the cigarettes.'

'But, Sir John, you told me not to give them to you?' I replied.

'GIVE ME THE FUCKING CIGARETTES, YOU LITTLE ARSEHOLE!!!' he roared.

Trembling (I can assure you!) I gave him the packet and he lit one up.

After a deep puff, he turned and stared at me – both barrels. 'I thought I told you not to give them to me?' he said. He then turned to the Master. 'Who is this fucking idiot? Why doesn't he do what he's fucking told? What the fuck are we doing employing an obvious idiot like that? Jesus fucking Christ!'

I slunk off and disappeared behind a deckhouse.

TRYING MY LUCK IN WELLINGTON

On those cargo ships I found a way of life that suited me and goals that got me motivated. After gaining the required four years' sea-time, my apprenticeship was over. Unfortunately that wasn't a qualification in itself. If I wanted to climb that totem pole, I'd have to knuckle down and find a Maritime College where I could study and qualify as a Second Mate. When I left school I was delighted to be leaving study behind, but having learned a touch more discipline and respect over the past few years, I was now ready to give it another shot.

Although my home port was still Melbourne, I had heard that the School of Navigation in Wellington, New Zealand, was a better place to study. Unlike Maritime schools in Australia at the time, which were run by institutes of technology, it was a standalone school established by seafarers solely for seafarers. Without a 'ticket' (a Certificate of Competency) the opportunities to work my way there were very limited, but I somehow managed to secure a bunk onboard a Union Company of New Zealand cargo ship as an unpaid, uncertificated fourth Mate – which was the lowest position you could get. This was on condition that I would work with the Company once I got my 'ticket'.

I hopped on my beaten-up old Triumph 650 motorbike and drove up to join the ship at North Wharf on the muddy Yarra River. As I headed to see the Master, I arranged for the surly Bosun (the leading sailor, a foreman of the unlicensed deck crew) to make sure the motorbike was loaded on deck. When we were ready to sail, I went down on deck and found a beautiful, brand new Honda 750/4 lashed down on deck, but my lowly Triumph was nowhere to be seen.

I got hold of the Bosun and learned that my bike was still on the wharf, and some other poor bastard's expensive pride and joy was just about to depart for New Zealand.

'Ah, fuck it,' said the Bosun. 'Just keep this one; no one will know in 15 minutes!'

Eventually, after a lot of cajoling from me, the very grumpy Bosun and his team of belligerent, half-pissed deckhands managed to re-rig the ship's derricks and change the bikes over just before sailing.

It was a miserable voyage across the Tasman in every respect. It was a crappy ship full of nasty people, and they made it very obvious they didn't want a fourth Mate onboard – especially not me. It was very rough, and with a lot of weight low down in the holds the little ship rolled heavily. The food was shithouse, the captain was pissed the whole time, and the gay cook and steward were acting just a little too nice (or so it seemed to me).

It was a great relief to finally roll into Wellington and make her fast. The Master was the first ashore, struggling with his rusty pushbike and clips on his trouser cuffs, leading the charge with the entire ship's complement in hot pursuit as he pedalled furiously for the nearest pub. Soon I was the only soul left onboard – a total ghost ship. I grabbed my bag and went ashore without a single glance back. There was no way I'd be returning to that ship after my study was done.

I had some time before school started up so I worked and travelled, blowing all my money in the usual ways. I wound up in Bluff, a shithole at the southernmost tip of New Zealand, where I got work in an abattoir. This led to a pivotal moment for me. It was 1969 and I was standing on the wharf, holding nothing but a plastic shopping bag and a toothbrush. A local wahine princess had cleaned me out of all my money and belongings – even my suitcase – and I was flat, penniless broke. Even the sight of Neil Armstrong hopping around on the surface of the moon earlier that day hadn't broken through my gloom.

I stared at the grey horizon and made a promise to myself that this would never, ever happen to me again. From that moment on I only ever looked ahead, and not astern.

From Bluff I 'ringbolted' (an old expression meaning 'travelled for free', from the days when discovered stowaways would be padlocked to a deck ringbolt), concealed by a sympathetic fellow seaman on an inter-island ferry back to Wellington, and thence to the imperious School of Navigation.

I finally started my studies and hit it off with one of my course-mates. He was a very large, hairy seafarer from Stornoway – a wild, windswept island off the west coast of Scotland – and he communicated in a series of grunts, growls, snorts, coughs and farts. We got along pretty well despite the fact I never understood a word he said. Occasionally a smile would appear, which was a trigger for me to smile back; otherwise I didn't have a clue what he was on about.

We moved into a flat together where we lived on beer and spaghetti bolognese. The big pot would stay on the stove for weeks at a time, and we'd just top it up with whatever crossed our paths – a partially eaten salad roll, cornflakes, whatever – and also stir in the brightly coloured mould that grew on the side of the pot. The lashings of Tui beer we guzzled must have staved off the food poisoning.

While I studied, I got a job via an agency on a ship that was salvaging the inter-island passenger ship *Wahine*. If a ship sinks and the insurers (in this case, Lloyds of London) pay out the claim, the wreck then becomes the property of the insurers and it's up to them to remove it and restore the seabed. Big insurers like Lloyds have their own salvage teams.

In this case, my father just happened to be the salvage ship's Master. He and my mum had divorced by this point and he had a new girlfriend in Wellington. This was an awkward coincidence, and Dad was taken completely by surprise. He didn't seem happy about it either, but I knew my stuff and the ship was hard up for experienced people willing to do this tough, dangerous, dirty job.

Everybody onboard knew that the Master was my dad, but he kept well away from me and I was soon accepted as one of the crowd. I mostly worked in the explosives magazine, which might sound important, but which in reality just involved cutting long cylinders of Semtex into four then rolling a condom onto each piece. (This was a much cheaper option than buying the pre-waxed explosives specifically designed for underwater use.) It was a shitty job that everyone else avoided, days spent ankle-deep in opened condom packets while the chemicals brought on a fearsome headache.

Aside from the Semtex headaches it was actually a great job compared to what I was used to by then: it was exciting, very dangerous and paid shitloads of money. I learned a lot from the deck crowd because only good seamen work on these kinds of ships. Their guiding principle for me was 'work hard and play harder', so it was difficult to juggle school as well as the hard, dangerous work and the totally obscene social life. But somehow I got through it all and emerged with a brand new Second Mate (Foreign-Going) Certificate of Competency. In effect, it was a ticket to the world – and in those days before Lonely Planet, the only people travelling the world were seafarers and adventurers.

Eventually my old man started making things difficult for me again. Not long after I got certificated as an officer (and apparently certified as a fool), a succession of fuck-ups on my part resulted in me being 'carpeted' before the Master on the salvage ship and effectively given the arse. Sacked. By my own father. It was time to move on.

Shortly after, I was offered a job by the owner of a small tug that was contracted to run all the scrap by barge from the salvage operation back into town. So I quickly got a Restricted Master's Certificate for the Port of Wellington and away I went – tug Master! My old man was furious when I turned up on the tug one morning in my new role. He glared at me most of the day.

On Fridays, the tug would leave with whichever of the salvage ship's crew members had the weekend off, and the instructions were very clear that the tug had to be away by 6pm on the dot to avoid any overtime penalty rates. I knew my old man was going ashore to see his girlfriend, and as the clock slowly moved towards six, I had the main engines started and the deckies out to slip the mooring lines. There were about half a dozen crew already onboard, all scrubbed up and in their weekend partying gear, but no sign of my old man.

Just as I was about to give the call, the Bosun and the leading diver stepped into the wheelhouse. 'Better wait for the old man,' they said (the Master on any ship is generally called 'the old man'). 'He'll be pissed off if we leave without him!'

'Fuck him, rules are rules. Let go fore and aft,' I called.

The Bosun and diver paled – they were terrified of my dad's foul temper. I walked the tug sideways off the salvage ship's side just as the old man burst out of the weather deck door, running down the deck with his shirt flying and clutching his weekend shag-bag.

'Hold that fucking tug,' he screamed.

'Get fucked,' I screamed back then and gave him the finger, a long blast on the whistle and a cheerful wave. He was stuck there for the whole weekend with only his foul mood for company. Nobody dared look at me on our very quiet trip back to town. In their eyes, I was a dead man walking.

I knew the longer I stuck around Wellington the more I was pushing my luck, so I cut my ties and aimed to make the most of my new ticket to the world. I had also had a girlfriend ashore, and she had moved into my little flat after the big hairy bear went back to Stornoway. But it was time to bid her farewell. I gave her my TV, furniture and fridge and took off – no regrets, no encumbrances, a pocket full of cash, and not a care in the world.

THE GIRLS FROM THE PURPLE ONION

The School of Navigation in Wellington, New Zealand was fantastic, and the principal, Captain Miller-Williams, knew exactly what to do with people like me. He was able to see through the bullshit and identify when someone had the goods to become a competent Mate and Master. I loved Captain Miller-Williams, in the truest form. He was a very special man.

He knew I was doing it hard: working as a shit-kicker on the salvage ship while partying as much as I could and studying at the same time. The salvage ship crowd were wild, tough sailors, and I learned some lifelong skills from them – and some bad habits, too! I developed a great respect for sailors who are masters of their craft.

The School of Navigation in Wellington always held a small Christmas party and made a point of inviting everyone of note in the maritime community. We were invited to bring along family and friends, particularly girlfriends and friends of girlfriends. My circle of girlfriends was small, but I wanted to help Captain Miller-Williams make the night a success.

One of the places we would crawl off to after a long day in the Royal Oak Hotel was the Purple Onion, a cabaret nightclub with expensive booze and a huge retinue of drag queens. So I asked them along. I advised Captain Miller-Williams that I had arranged for some extra girls to join us, and he was very pleased.

The party started on time in the rooms of the college and the grog was flowing, but I was a little dismayed to see how many old farts – old examiners of Masters and Mates (whom we greatly feared), crusty old surveyors, old marine pilots, old local politicians and board members – were there.

Just as I was beginning to have second thoughts about my plan for the girls from the Purple Onion, the door burst open, and in walked eight of the most sensationally dressed, everything hanging out, thigh-high skirted, high-heeled 'girls' you'd ever seen. Things sparked up very quickly; the old guys were into it in a flash, and the girls lapped up the attention.

Captain Miller-Williams glided past, so I pulled him alongside and 'fessed up. As I revealed who the girls really were, and where they had come from, the colour drained from his face and his jaw dropped to the floor. He looked at me, then at the senior members of Wellington's maritime community (now pissed) draped in feather boas, with gaudy lipstick kisses on their cheeks, and said, 'Well done – that's a pass!'

A SPLASH OF COLOUR

There is nothing glamorous about salvage work, and our ship in Wellington was typically filthy. Not because it was neglected – far from it. Rather, it was because everything that was brought up from the wreck was covered in the growth, mud, oil and general shit that builds after a year on the seabed.

But the interior was a different matter. No work clothes or dirty boots were allowed inside, and everything was as neat and tidy as possible. We had a good cook, a gay chief steward and a big transgender steward who looked after us very well. They'd all camp it up a bit, especially when I was around as they could see the terrified look on my face. The meals were excellent and there'd always be cakes and stuff at smoko. Plus there seemed to be fresh flowers everywhere, which was unusual for a working ship but gave the place a homely feel that everyone appreciated.

One Friday, we were all invited to a party at the apartment these three shared together. They really turned it on and there was plenty of fine food and lashings of grog. I spotted the Bosun near a window having a smoke and popped over to say hello.

'Know where we are?' he asked.

'Nup, wouldn't have a fucking clue,' I said.

'Well, over there, just across the road, is the cemetery,' said the Bosun. 'And a short walk further down is the little jetty where we pick up everyone on Monday morning in the workboat.'

'Yeah, and …?'

'Well, where do you think all the flowers come from?' said the Bosun.

It turned out that every Monday, these three – which included a rough-looking, unshaven trans woman in a miniskirt and high heels – would wander through the cemetery grabbing all the fresh flowers they could carry. Somehow, the flowers throughout the ship didn't seem quite so homely after that.

HOME FOR CHRISTMAS

I returned home for Christmas after several years at sea. By then in my 20s, I was a different guy. I'd seen a lot and done a lot – both good and bad – and had spent time with a lot of seafarers – good, bad and dangerous. No longer a pudgy schoolboy, I was hardened beyond my years and had learned to manage my fears. I walked with a confidence that only a seafarer knows: not scared of the shadows, but always tense and alert.

The family home, which I loved so dearly, looked very different. I felt uncomfortable, partly because I was smoking by this stage and had to work hard at not swearing so readily. I could see the look of horror cross my mother's face whenever I dropped a clanger! My father had also decided to come home for Christmas. I wasn't intimidated by him anymore, which clearly made him uncomfortable. A showdown seemed inevitable and it came on Christmas Day, fuelled by grog and inflamed by years of abuse towards both me and my mother.

Perhaps I had subconsciously encouraged the confrontation; I can't exactly remember what the trigger was, but the trigger was pulled – well and truly. But Dad hadn't accounted for the fact that I'd graduated from a hard school these last few years; no Marquess of Queensberry Rules for me – get in hard and fast and don't stop. It was over in a moment, and although I'd won Round 1, I could see there was more to come. I jumped on my motorcycle, an old 250 trail bike, and lit off into the night. No belongings, no money and definitely, in those days, no credit cards or phone. I had to drain the last squirts of petrol left in the hoses at the now-closed petrol stations, got to a friend's place and stayed on his sofa.

When I rang home several days later, I learned that my father had left – he never returned home again.

MADE TO ORDER

I was a brand new, first-trip Third Mate on a cargo ship in Hong Kong. Having spent five years as an indentured apprentice, the lowest form of marine growth, I had started making some serious money for the first time in my life.

In those days the cargo ships at Hong Kong would stay secured to mooring buoys out in the harbour because there was no wharf space alongside. It was no big deal; we were all used to it. There were always bum-boats to hire to get ashore if you needed it, but many vendors would simply come out and set up shop on the ship. There was always a 'sew sew', usually an older Chinese woman who would sew your buttons back on, hem your strides or whatever, and a tailor or two would often come aboard to drum up business.

One time I got cornered by a shirt tailor that I just couldn't shake off. One of the engineers came past and vouched for the tailor, so I agreed to let him measure me for some short-sleeved shirts. I chose about eight different checks and colours and was feeling pretty swish. But several days later, as it came close to sailing time, there was no sign of my newly tailored shirts.

At the very last minute, to my relief, the tailor hustled aboard and delivered my new shirts. They were all nicely wrapped in cellophane, with cardboard at the back and under the collar, and one sleeve folded across the front. Beautiful! I paid him and we set sail.

Off we went, north from Hong Kong, to Taiwan then to several ports in Japan. It was freezing cold so there was definitely no need for a short-sleeved shirt. Then we got to Agana in Guam, where it was warmer and we got a chance for a run ashore and a few beers. So I grabbed one of my new shirts from the drawer and opened it up only to find that there was just the front of the shirt and one sleeve folded across it – nothing else. Every shirt!

Lesson learned, but I did have some fun when I got back home to Melbourne and surprised my friends with the gift of a nice new shirt for Christmas.

BUYING A HONDA
IN TOKYO

One of the perks of travelling on a ship is that it's easy to take home big souvenirs – like motorbikes.

Japan was the place. There is a huge area in the Tokyo suburb of Ueno full of second-hand motorcycles at ridiculously cheap prices, and we would head there with a pocket full of cash to bag a bargain.

It was common for ten or more motorbikes to come onboard, and even non-motorcyclists would take the opportunity to grab a bargain. The weapon of choice, in those days, was a Honda 750/4. Quite a machine in its day, and still a head-turner today.

I had always been a motorcyclist and slowly built my cash bag up to be able to buy a brand new one from the big, flash Honda dealer in Tokyo. It was exciting to go to this big store and pick one off the elevated display area. There was a large aisle with a long red carpet down the middle with rows of pot plants and all the motorcycles on display on each side.

After I made my choice and paid the cash, the dealer explained that it would take a few hours to prepare it and do the pre-delivery. When I returned, I could see my new Honda ready to go, and the dealer standing there with all the books and paperwork. He was very unhappy that I was planning to ride this unregistered, uninsured bike back to the port, but had resigned himself to the thought that the problem, if there were one, would be mine and not his.

He politely asked if I was familiar with the bike and this particular very powerful model.

'No problem,' I said, and gave him the universal thumbs up.

He didn't look totally convinced. Justifiably so, as, in fact, I had never ridden one of these bikes in my life – but, no need for him to know that.

I jumped aboard and fired her up – fantastic! But I popped the clutch a bit too soon and suddenly all hell broke loose. It took me a few seconds to figure out what was happening. It seemed the massive torque to the rear wheel had picked up the red carpet on the aisle, and it was disappearing out the back wheel at 160 kilometres per hour, bringing with it a stream of pot plants on either side. When the carpet ran out and the now nicely heated rear tyre hit the concrete, I took off down the aisle at high speed, through the double doors and out across four lanes of high-density Tokyo traffic, then stalled it.

Fortunately, Japanese drivers are excellent, and a motorbike jumping out of a showroom in front of them without warning was the kind of thing they took in their stride. Not so, the dealer and his staff, who were still crawling out of the wreckage of red carpet and pot plants. I made a hasty escape.

SANTA'S ZIP-LINE

The ship was a cargo liner – much like a standard cargo ship but with a lot more accommodation for fare-paying passengers. It was a lovely ship in every respect, and I loved my job as Second Mate. As it was not a full-blown passenger ship, with all the services and distractions these ships carry, it was up to all onboard to help out with the guests wherever possible – especially when it came to entertainment.

There were many children on this Christmas voyage, so the officers decided it would be a bit of fun to have Santa drop into the children's play area via a zip-line. No problem. Any competent seafarer should be able to rig up a wire and a Bosun's chair. As for Santa, one engineer officer was substantial in both beard and girth, so that was easy. He may not have been the most pleasant of characters – he was a typical world traveller, and one who hadn't had much exposure to children – but at least he fit the physical requirements.

A long wire was rigged up by the crew, which went from the funnel deck four decks down to the railing just above the children's play area. As it was a pretty steep angle, the Chief

Mate decided to leave a bit of slack in the wire to slow the rate of descent. The corpulent engineer officer was fitted out with a pretty flash Santa suit, and his beard was recoloured to match. As there was no time for a test flight, it was left up to the Chief Mate and his worldly experience to get the numbers right.

The afternoon arrived, and all hands were summoned to the funnel deck to help prepare the missile. There was a problem getting the engineer's arse into the Bosun's chair, and the zip-line drooped alarmingly as it took his considerable weight. A large sack of presents was passed to him, some final adjustments made to beard and gear, and a mighty push sent him on his way.

In hindsight, perhaps the mighty push was a bit overdone …

As Santa dropped down a deck at a fantastic speed, he let out a mighty 'FUUUUUCK!!!!' Still accelerating past the next two decks, much to the alarm of passengers enjoying a drink there, he screamed as the Bosun's chair, and Santa's arse, hit the railing, sending him into a spin.

With another mighty 'FUUUCK!!' Santa jettisoned the sack of toys, which struck two passengers asleep in deckchairs, then hit the deck with a ferocious screech as the zip-line, it was now clear, was far too slack to get him to his target.

Santa left a large, 2-metre-long red skid mark on the deck as he smashed through the waiting parents and children. He took out all the chairs and tables – not to mention the Christmas tree – shedding his boots, pants and jacket as he went, and then ended up in a screaming heap against the railing.

As the parents rescued their distressed and injured children to assess the damage (both physical and psychological), our Santa, now down to his boxer shorts, limped off to the stairway screaming, 'You can all go and get fucked!'

Not quite the result expected.

BURIED AT SEA

I worked on a fair few passenger–cargo ships over the years. Even though it was a relatively expensive way to travel, and it took quite a bit of time to get anywhere because the ship would also load and unload cargo along the way, the passengers loved it. It was a chance for them to become part of the working ship.

The passengers who had the time and money for such travel were often old, sometimes very old, and inevitably a few would cark it along the way. Fortunately these kinds of ships always had a doctor onboard, which meant that a death certificate could be issued and a sea burial could be offered as an alternative to freighting the body home. Once the next-of-kin learned the costs involved in freighting a body from a foreign port, the sea burial usually looked pretty attractive.

Sea burials run to a format. The ship is stopped in the water at sunrise. The body is prepared in a canvas-weighted shroud, which is then placed on a polished wooden plank and covered with a flag. One end of the table is hinged on the ship's rail, and the other end is held by an officer on either side. The flag is secured at the inboard end, and once the Master completes the service, he nods to the officers, they lift up the plank and the weighted body shoots out from underneath the flag, over the side and into the drink. Easy. What could possibly go wrong …?

On one particular voyage we had a run of dead bodies, and as the Second Mate on the 12–4am watch, with each new death I had to stay awake after my watch ended at 4am to do the deed at sunrise. I was getting pretty pissed off, to be honest, and when yet another old man died unexpectedly, I suggested to the Mate that maybe it was about time the engineer officers coming off watch at 4am could take charge of a burial or two. He agreed, and the engineer officers were ordered to make themselves available

That morning, at 4am, the two engineer officers came out of the hot engine room, had a shower and grabbed a beer – usual practice. One asked the other if he'd ever performed a sea burial before.

'No,' the other officer replied, 'but it can't be too difficult if those dickhead bridge officers can do it.'

So they went down to take a look at the setup, beers in hand. The ship was travelling along at full speed in the darkness, and the body was laid out all ready to go: shroud, plank, flag and all. In an hour or so, just before sunrise, the ship would stop and the dead man's grieving wife, along with the Master, would arrive for the burial ceremony.

'Grab an end, let's see how heavy it is,' said one to the other.

Not very heavy at all, they found out, as the body shot from under the flag, over the rail and into the sea at 18 knots.

That's a fuck-up.

Being good engineers, they went back to the bar and cracked another beer. Eventually, they roused the Mate, who sat bolt upright and let out a mighty 'WTF!' All hands were mustered: the ship's carpenter, butcher, engineers, doctor and anyone else in striking distance. Soon a 2-metre-long 'body' was hastily made up from the best parts of a sheep carcass, a few engine-room spares, and other odds and ends – just in time, as the engines slowed and the ship glided to a stop.

The new widow emerged from her cabin. The captain solemnly read the service and gave the nod, and the engineer officers lifted the plank. There was a thunderous roar as 250 kilograms of carcass and scrap metal went over the side like a fucking missile.

The widow looked a bit startled; her recently deceased husband had been quite a small, slim man …

A FIERY AFFAIR

On passenger ships, officers were expected to mingle with and entertain the passengers – which we got very good at.

One evening as Second Mate, I was just about to head for the bridge to stand the 12–4am watch when the fire alarm sounded. Fire alarms are always taken seriously, on every ship, and by every person. As I opened the door to the bridge, the Chief Mate hurtled out, yelling, 'Chief engineer's cabin!'

There was a stampede as the fire party followed in hot pursuit and flung open the cabin door to be greeted by a waft of black smoke. Standing there with a very surprised look on his face was the chief engineer, fanning a wet towel at a startled older lady in a smouldering dress.

WTF.

The Chief Mate moved quickly, and once he was sure that the fire was out, he handed the woman off to the ship's nurse and doctor. The suddenly sheepish chief engineer had some questions to answer, but it was a few days before the truth filtered down. A notorious lecher with a penchant for older women, the chief engineer had wheeled the woman up to his cabin for a bit of one-on-one entertaining. She'd had a few too many drinks and passed out in the evening chair, and the chief engineer had decided to lift up her dress – and, unfortunately for all, used his cigarette lighter to illuminate the scene. And up she went.

Fortunately the fabric flashed off pretty quick, and the chief had an ice bucket and water jug handy – very professional.

We never heard what the outcome was, nor what explanation had been offered, but the lady stayed onboard for the remainder of the voyage and seemed to have a wonderful time. Although she steered well clear of the chief engineer.

A ROYAL TURD

I was at the Ocean Terminal in Hong Kong when one of the engineers came running up to tell me that the famous ship *Gothic* was alongside. He wanted to take me over there for a few beers and a big surprise.

We made our way over to the other side of the terminal and there was the majestic *Gothic*, the Shaw, Savill & Albion cargo–passenger ship that had been used by the newly crowned Queen Elizabeth on her 1954 coronation world cruise (and was later converted back to a normal cargo/passenger configuration).

My engineer mate knew his way around the ship, and we shot straight up to the officer's bar just in time for lunchtime drinks, which lasted five hours – by which point it was time for the big surprise.

Someone produced a key with a fancy tag and opened up a cabinet about the size of a dartboard cabinet. Inside was a sealed glass tube mounted on a wooden bracket – and contained inside was a bronzed turd. A very, very special turd. A Queen Elizabeth II Royal Turd, no less!

So the story goes, the engineers onboard *Gothic* during the Royal Tour had blanked off and diverted the toilet line from Her Majesty's crapper, and trapped a royal turd. This was then preserved, bronzed, sealed in a glass tube and kept under lock and key, only to be displayed when three or more people agreed to open the cabinet.

Gothic is now long gone, scrapped in the 70s, but I wonder where the Royal Turd ended up – Greenwich Maritime Museum perhaps? Wherever it is, I hope the keeper of the turd still maintains the three-person rule, which seems the height of decorum.

HATCH BROTHERS EMPORIUM

Shipping containers dominate the industry now. Every bit of cargo you could imagine can now be stowed in a container of some sort. But that wasn't always the case. Indeed, before 1955, *all* cargo was shipped in boxes, bags, cartons, crates, and bales, and that approach was still very common well into my first years at sea.

Piece by piece the cargo would be swung onboard from the wharf, then lowered through the hatch and down into the holds. The wharfies would then stow and stack each article, which required a fair bit of skill. Ship's officers would be on duty all the time, checking that cargo was stowed in the correct order in the correct hatch and hold for later discharge, and that no pilfering took place.

This was pretty much wishful thinking, though, with one officer watching six hatches being loaded simultaneously by six gangs of wharfies in a dark and dingy cargo hold. Theft was rife.

Eventually the cargo would be loaded, the hatches closed and the ship would sail for the next port. Along the way, the crew would clean everything up and check that the cargo was secure and undamaged. Of course, each hatch, hold and 'tween deck (the space in between decks in each hold) was an Aladdin's cave of treasures and delights. All manner of prizes could be discovered by tearing a little hole in a cardboard box and sticking your hand in for a lucky dip. Cargo coming into Australia from South-East Asia was always particularly interesting to the crew – especially anything marked 'GJC'. That indicated a shipment from GJ Coles, which imported every item you could think of: toys, clothes, shoes, tools, the lot. This custom gave rise to the famous, amongst seamen at least, 'Hatch Brothers Emporium'.

On one memorable occasion when I was Third Mate on a cargo ship returning from Japan, I was on the bridge when I noticed the Chinese deck crew turn-to on deck. All ten of them were dressed in the same worn and dirty shirts and dungarees – and the same brightly coloured sports shoes in the latest fashion. This kind of thing was a fairly common sight, though sometimes it was shirts or even faux-fur coats.

Shippers started trying to thwart the Hatch Brothers Emporium with various ruses, such as packing all of the left shoes in one box, and all of the right shoes in another – different sizes, different styles and different colours all mixed up. That was no problem, though – it just meant that more boxes had to be ripped open until a matching pair (or close to a matching pair) could be found.

Thankfully, for the commercial world, in 1956 a truckie from North Carolina named Malcolm McLean created the shipping container for his own company SeaLand. Hand-loading a ship cost $5.86 a ton at that time, but using containers would make it cost only 16 cents a ton to load a ship. The concept took off, and by the late 1960s it had totally killed off the general cargo ships, which were replaced with sleek, efficient and totally soulless container ships.

From then on, the goods were sealed in steel shipping containers, stowed very close together so their doors couldn't be opened at sea. This solved the pilfering problem onboard the ships but not elsewhere. Thieves and crooks ashore now just stole the whole container – made it a lot easier all 'round!

This totally killed it for me, too. I lasted a year or so on container ships, but it was no place for me – time to look around.

THE PATCH

It was a bit of a shock to the system when I found myself on an anchor-handling supply vessel (AHSV), servicing a huge oil rig in 'The Patch' (as the Bass Strait Oilfields are known) in the middle of a fierce winter gale. The main role of these ships was to move the enormous anchors of the oil rig into position, but we also shipped supplies in from land and towed the rig itself when required. The tough, powerful little ship could have easily fitted on the foredeck of my last ship.

Roll, pitch, yaw, sway, heave – every axis was active, usually all at the same time, and I was very, very crook. Only seamen who really enjoyed their profession came to work on these ships; everyone else stayed on the bulk carriers and container ships, swinging on the end of a mop or a paintbrush.

I was the Mate on this ship, but I knew fuck all about the job – I'd never seen anything like it in my life! Fortunately for me, good seamen are good blokes, and they looked after me and taught me well. I was a good student. I loved the hard physical work, the excitement and danger, and the back-to-basics sailorising.

Did I mention danger? This was real bum-clenching danger, whereas the most danger you might have encountered on my last ship, a passenger ship, was a handsy widow on the dance floor!

I had never worked so hard physically as I did in that ship. We worked around the clock, on everything and anything the rig required: pulling anchors, running anchors, connecting tow wires, static towing, and running supplies, stores, fuel, bulk cement and anything else they could dream up. All of this was done in some of the worst conditions you will find anywhere in the world. Gale-force winds, huge seas and swell, and the little ship never stopped rolling and heaving.

The food supplied was plentiful and excellent quality but there was no cook to cook it. Instead, one of the ABs would dash off the deck and into the galley and knock up whatever he could in what little time he had to spare from his duties out on deck.

They would all start off with good intentions, armed with a bunch of recipes from home with lengthy instructions from their wives, but it never took long to turn to shit. You'd think it was impossible to fuck up spaghetti bolognese, but it can be done! Cooking for eight hungry men is a big job, but doing it in a galley that's leaping up and down 3 metres, and continuously rolling and pitching is not exactly *MasterChef* conditions. Toast and cheese became very popular.

The early ships were basic: two fixed blade propellers in Kort nozzles, twin ganged rudders, and one bowthruster.

The Master did all the 'driving', and the ship-handling skills of an experienced offshore Master were second to none. It's not something you can learn from a book, and has to be instinctive. If you had to stop and think about it, you'd fail.

As US Navy Commander Ernest King famously said, 'The mark of a great ship handler is never getting in situations that require great ship-handling.'

I was lucky because the Masters I first sailed with were great drivers and willing to let me have a go. This was easier said than done, because every manoeuvre was 'on the job', so the clients were watching and always very critical of any fuck-up. (A novice driver tearing the side out of a rig or destroying a critical wharf would be classed as a fuck-up!) I loved driving, and you had to love it or you'd *never* be good at it.

So I did my first four weeks in The Patch and was nearly a fully fledged 'Bass Strait Scaly-Back'. I got my seasickness under control, and didn't shit my pants *every* time a 60-millimetre wire let go and went twanging past my ear. I learned to swear properly and to drink gallons of beer at the Welshpool Pub, and gained a few muscles.

It was a good feeling to step ashore and head home – the job satisfaction was huge. But safely ashore and home, the doubts crept in. Fucking dangerous, hard, uncomfortable – hmmmm, not so sure if I really wanted to go back.

Then my wife-to-be mentioned that there was a mistake with my pay; some computer cock-up had resulted in a shitload of money being deposited into my account. I rang the office and they were onto it in a flash. After a lot of muttering and calculating, the guy came back and said that everything was in order: my different bonuses and allowances had all been paid correctly. And there was another bucketload of cash being paid in that day.

I quietly hung up the phone and told my fiancée I'd go back for another swing and see how it went; I'd never been paid so much money in my life! Cash is a great cure for seasickness, and I was still there 12 years later!

SETTLING DOWN (ALMOST)

I'd got to a stage in life, around when I left the container ships and started working in offshore oil, when I realised I was lonely. Sure, I had people around me all the time, but I didn't really have a strong connection to my family and I was envious of those that did. It dawned on me that I should make an effort to make my own family.

I'd had a long relationship with a girl, a nurse, whom I was quite convinced I would marry – but, most unexpectedly, she fucked off with a fellow (male) nurse instead. I later found out they were serious users of prescription medication and other drugs. Three months after she dumped me, she was found on Rottnest Island, dead in bed from a drug overdose. That made it pretty final!

So I drifted between jobs for a few years, living pretty wild but not very happy.

I bumped into my current (and only) wife, Sandy, in between my wild journeys around the world. We'd grown up in the same neighbourhood and were good mates who had known each other for nearly ten years, but had never gone out together and had different friendship groups. Beaumaris was a pretty bushy, wild place in those days, and I remembered she'd always ridden a white horse everywhere, even to the private school she attended. The last time we'd met she'd been engaged, and I'd been pretty close to it, too. But now we both had disastrous stories – mine was dead, and hers had turned out to be a heavy drinker with a nasty streak.

Talk about a rebound!

It was quite an easy relationship to step into because we were friends. She had a good job and was paying off a small house on Beach Road, Black Rock. (Wish we had it now!) I'd been staying with her for a month when she told me that I should pick up all my stuff and move in properly. She looked a bit disappointed when I told her I already had. All I had to my name were three pairs of jeans, six T-shirts, a box of photo albums and a fucked motorcycle – I got the impression she'd been expecting more …

TOOLS OF THE TRADE

A knife and a spike are the true emblems of a sailor who takes pride in his profession, the traditional tools of the trade that are fast disappearing. In the days of sail, a seaman wouldn't dare consider joining a ship without this equipment. He'd be expected to show them to the Mate when he stepped aboard, and if his deck knife had a sharp point on the end of its blade then he'd be sent along to see the ship's carpenter, who would use a cold chisel to chop the end off. A proper deck knife always had a squared-off end; a sharp end is of no use on the deck of a ship, except to stick into someone else's guts in a fight.

The knives and spikes were always of a 'handy' size so as to be used aloft; this was no place for big showy combat knives or farmers' sheath knifes. They usually had a small wrist lanyard, so if they accidentally slipped from your grip they wouldn't fall and kill someone on deck below. They were valuable, especially to people who were paid shit wages, and they were frequently made onboard with a high level of artistry, as there was always plenty of time on a long ocean voyage.

When I first went to sea on cargo ships you were still expected to have a knife and a spike; I proudly wore mine on a strong leather belt and felt undressed without it, although they were never worn ashore. Mine had been stowed away in a cupboard for years once I became an officer on conventional ships, but as Mate on an AHSV I wore them again with pride.

The crews on anchor clankers were small in those days: Master and Mate, two engineers, and four ABs. It was essential for the Mate to be working on deck with the ABs, as the workload was huge and the operation went 24 hours a day. The engineers were stretched, too, as one of them was always required on deck to drive the massive diesel-powered towing/work winch while the other engineer would be down below in the immaculately clean engine room keeping everything running at full noise. The knife and spike were critically important on the work deck: instant decisions had to be made to cut gear away or whip out a shackle split pin; running around the deck like a headless chook trying to find tools was totally unacceptable.

With the Mate working on deck, the Master was alone on the bridge doing all the driving; there was no one else onboard qualified to stand a watch and give them a break. After a long, hard day's work on deck, the Mate would crawl up to the bridge and relieve the Master, who would try to grab something to eat and a bit of rest. Then the sea-watches would start for the run back to port, and only the Master and Mate were certificated watchkeepers – six hours on and six hours off, day after day for eight weeks. But no one ever complained; our wages were four times what we would have been paid on a conventional ship, and we got seven months' leave a year.

Over time, a great camaraderie would develop between the eight crew members, such was the intensity of the work and the reliance on one another. There would often be very little said when working on deck because each person knew what the other was doing or about to do. If you needed a hammer, there was one in your hand automatically. Some of the jobs were very dangerous and only a fool wouldn't be scared, but being scared was healthy, and the best way of staying alive.

A Mate would be on deck for several years before he would ever be considered for a Master's job, which ensured that every Master knew the dangers faced and effort expected of those working on deck – how one push of the wrong lever, or a moment's inattention, could sweep a 100-millimetre steel cable across the deck and kill everyone instantly.

The crews were always very proud of their skilful Master, and equally and cruelly critical of anyone they found to be lacking. It was a thin line, because one small mistake could instantly and irreversibly change the Master's status from peacock to feather duster.

The worst insult was to be called a 'farmer' – the most useless fucker one could ever have onboard a working ship (sailors who also happened to own farms were the only exception).

As the years rolled on, the industry exploded and changed, sometimes for the better, but not always. The crews got bigger, and technology made the work safer and easier. We got a cook – a professional one – and dined like kings. (On two occasions I had owner-chefs from Michelin three-star restaurants work onboard – they told me the workload was easier and the pay was better!) A Second Mate also appeared – what a luxury! Now the Master and Mate could get decent rest and find time for a proper meal. More importantly, there was now someone to process the mountains of paperwork we were starting to get buried under.

But the wrong types of seamen started coming into the industry. There were simply not enough willing and able seamen to fill the jobs, and when word got out about the film-star pay, every mop-swinging, paintbrush-wielding crew-bar prop drifted across. And instead of a knife and spike, they'd come fully rigged with an iPhone and bluetooth headset. Most couldn't tie their own shoelaces, let alone a bowline, and always had a pocket full of cable ties and gaffer tape. WTF. They used words like 'left' and 'right'; 'floors', 'ceilings', 'walls', 'front' and 'back'. Words like 'port', 'starboard', 'decks', 'deckheads', 'bulkheads', 'fore' and 'aft' were a mystery to them.

This also included some of the Second Mates who started appearing, and they seemed more interested in computer software than the functionality of a working ship. Changes in sea service requirements for certificates of competency soon meant we had all sorts coming in. One new officer had spent most of his time driving a glass-bottom boat around a reef resort, while others came from 'white boats' (billionaires' luxury yachts) in the Mediterranean.

Finally, and this seemed like the final straw for some, we started to see more women at sea, which turned out to be pretty uneventful despite the dire predictions of shore staff. They were welcome so long as they pulled their weight, did their job, and fitted in with everyone – which, in my experience, was always the case. They worked hard and smart, were always reliable and polite, and didn't run ashore and get pissed at every available opportunity.

A lot of the dangerous practices and techniques we'd all taken for granted quietly disappeared and a new species of animal arrived on the scene: an occupational health and safety manager, armed to the teeth with safety procedures and a risk analysis matrix, but little experience of the sea beyond an afternoon jet-skiing in Bali. WTF.

The very first safety manager I ever saw came onboard an anchor-handler operating in Bass Strait to 'get an understanding' of the risks involved. After five sleepless days and nights of horrendous weather and heavy seas; listening to the constant roar of engines, thrusters and winches; and observing (from the safe and warm confines of the wheelhouse) men being swept up the deck by 'greenies' as heavy wires and chains parted on an hourly basis, he was clearly terrified. He scrambled ashore and took off in his car without a murmur, never to be seen again. We did get one recommendation from him though – perhaps the cook should wear boots in the galley? Thanks for your professional input!

Safety helmets were introduced, jeans and footy socks were replaced with fluoro overalls, and thongs were definitely banned! Even pull-on boots went west and had to be replaced with lace-up boots. Deck crews didn't want lace-up boots at all; they *needed* pull-on boots so they could kick them off in an instant when they got swept overboard and had to swim for their lives in the freezing cold waters of Bass Strait.

Then, one of these industry experts had a lightbulb moment and concluded that knives were extremely dangerous things, particularly those very sharp and menacing knives that sailors swaggered around with on their belts like Pirates of the Caribbean. All incidents and accidents involving knives, no matter how minor, were logged, including any that occurred in ships' galleys to people involved in food preparation – which seemed imbalanced. No experienced sailor could recall anyone on deck ever seriously cutting himself with a deck knife; there were plenty of other things to be found on deck that would cut your finger, or more probably rip your fucking arm off.

But the experts weren't interested, and knives were banned. I was Master of a big, sophisticated Norwegian -flag ship working under contract in the oilfields when the ban was introduced. On the first day, the contractor's safety officer spotted an evil sailor swaggering around deck with a murderous knife on his belt. 'Jesus H Christ, shut the job down!' the safety officer screamed.

A hasty meeting was called and work would not proceed until the culprit was caught, manacled and thrashed. The million-dollar-a-day contract was suspended until the matter could be resolved, and my company was furious with the delay. An urgent investigation found that the Bosun was the evil culprit.

I knew him well, and counted him as a friend. He was a highly experienced, very professional seaman, held in high regard by all who knew him, and I considered it a luxury to have someone of his calibre onboard my ship. He knew how to manage a big staff of seamen and was utterly responsible, trustworthy and reliable in every way, at all times polite and well presented, passionate about his profession and a good shipmate in every respect. He was also a strong and staunch SUA man (Seaman's Union of Australia), but with a balanced set of values, and I had always found him to be fair and reasonable to deal with. He had a knife and spike on his belt because these were essential tools of his trade, and I cited numerous instances in which people were saved from death or serious injury because someone was able to quickly cut them away.

The contractor's manager wouldn't budge, and I steadfastly refused to allow my men on deck without these tools. We now had a deadlock.

My Bosun was eventually and begrudgingly given a special dispensation from the contractor's policies, which had to be renewed daily, to carry a deck knife while working on deck. The world was changing, and it was the first time I really felt that myself and my breed of seafarers were no longer fitting in.

On the third day of this new regime, one of the contractor's men had his shirtsleeve snagged by a wire jag on a 35-tonne work winch and was being quickly dragged into the revolving winch drum. Once wrapped up in the winch drum, he'd be dog meat. Our Bosun, conditioned to having his eyes everywhere and constantly alert to every risk, took one quick step, whipped out his deck knife and instantly cut him free. Nobody said a word, but management looked pretty sheepish peering out from under their shiny company safety helmets.

BONGO VAN

Work in the Bass Strait Oilfields was always cold, hard and dangerous, so we'd all look forward to a return to port and a run to the pub. The problem was that the nearest pub to port was in Toora about 15 kilometres away.

On one particular day, after work had finished, we rushed ashore and piled into one of the crew members' rusty, beaten-up Bongo van. There were a couple of ships in port so it was a bit of a squeeze for the ten of us in the tiny van – three crammed into the front, and the rest standing up in the back like vertical sardines.

The little Bongo van struggled with the big load, but once clear of the security checkpoint boom gate we gathered momentum befitting such an important mission. Pulling up outside the pub, we jumped, crawled and fell out of the mighty Bongo, which we then discovered had developed a serious problem: the accelerator cable, linking the pedal to the motor in the back, had broken, and although the engine would idle fine, it couldn't be revved up. No problem; 'worry about it later' was the cry as we all stampeded into the bar of the small country hotel.

It was a great session and a good time was had by all – especially the publican, who made more in one night of our patronage than in a month with only the tight-arse local farmers. But it was going to be a very slow ride back in the Bongo with no accelerator.

Mazda Bongo vans have the engine in the back. To access the engine, you lift open the tailgate and then there is a little hatch lid in the floor that allows you to see into the engine space. I was always pretty handy around cars and discovered that if I sat at the back and kept the lid open, I could just reach in and adjust the throttle linkage by hand. All we needed was a signal system between the driver – another Master and good mate of mine – and me. Easy: one bang on the roof to accelerate, two bangs to slow down. So, with much shouting and yelling, we blasted off.

Unfortunately, the signal system was a bit drowned out by the yelling and screaming, so the gear changes were a bit messy. The first corner was taken way too fast for the heavily laden Bongo. As we approached another very dangerous corner, I heard the two bangs on the roof warning me to decelerate. But I decided to ignore it and keep the hammer down – just for fun.

The driver stared in horror at the fast-approaching corner, the crowd screamed their approval, and the Bongo slid into the turn at race pace.

But our coach captain wasn't up to it, and halfway through the corner he jumped on the brakes. Now, the brakes of this van could barely even trigger the brake lights – and that's on a good day. In terror, the driver turned off the ignition key, which instantly resulted in three high-risk changes: the headlights went out so the dangerous corner disappeared into darkness; the rear wheels dragged so the Bongo began to fishtail dramatically; and the steering wheel locked. The pissed-up Bongo sardines in the back roared their approval at this escalation in risk, even more so when our coach captain restarted the engine. At that moment the unburned fuel in the manifold exploded with a mighty bang and the headlights came back to spotlight the impending disaster. Fortunately the steering wheel unlocked too, and traction was restored. Away we went again with a mighty roar of support from all aboard.

The next obstacle was the port security gate where the boom was down awaiting our arrival and inspection.

I cranked the throttle wide open as we lined up for the boom gate. A terrified, and fortunately sober, security guard leaped for the boom gate and managed to flip it up in time as the Bongo flashed through. The crowd roared louder still!

The darkened hull of our ship showed up in the headlights, and with a demonstration of great skill, the driver threw the Bongo into a picture perfect rally-car slide and pulled up right next to the gangway in a shower of gravel and mud. The passengers all roared, pouring out of the steaming Bongo after a lovely, relaxing night ashore.

THE LEGEND OF GEOFF

Before pirates became fashionable, Geoff was the archetype. He had weathered, hawk-like features with a dramatic widow's peak and a gold earring the size of a shower-curtain ring. He had a very loud, deep, gravelly voice brought about by years of continuous cigar smoking and heavy drinking, and his swearing would make a wharfie blush. Geoff always had a good story: for him, life was one never-ending adventure. He was also first-class seaman, a natural-born ship handler and a joy to watch in action.

I was lucky enough to sail as Mate with Geoff in the Bass Strait Oilfields on an anchor-handling supply vessel (AHSV), when the industry was still new and a little unregulated. The work was very tough, very dangerous and very uncomfortable – Bass Strait isn't a nice place. But Geoff had it nailed. He had a state-of-the-art ship, all the latest gear and a very powerful, close-knit crew. It was exciting to become a part of it and, eventually, to become accepted as a member.

These ships, like the whole offshore drilling industry, were totally dry – no alcohol at sea. At all, ever. There was no place on the deck, engine room or bridge for anyone to be handicapped by the piss. But once the ship was tied up at the wharf with the main engines shut down, all hell would break loose – and in the lead, always, was Geoff.

With an ever-present cigar, he was a formidable sight as he fronted the bar. Did I mention he could fight? It was all the more confronting because Geoff was a little oddly rigged. While his right arm was enormous and immensely powerful, his left – always encased in a long sleeve – was withered and small. As a very young deck boy in the late 1950s, while crossing the Bay of Biscay on a general cargo ship, Geoff was fucking about when he slipped and fell over the side. The ship continued and left him treading water in the wake. Fortunately, someone saw Geoff go and raised the alarm; the ship slowly turned around and backtracked to find him.

It's very difficult to spot a man's head bobbing around in the water, especially if there are a few white caps, and especially at twilight. Geoff was relieved to see the ship turn around but now he had a whole new problem to deal with: as the ship approached and slowed down, the bright cargo lights attracted a large school of voracious barracuda. And Geoff was on the menu.

He never saw them coming; he felt the first one when it hit him at great speed. Within seconds they were tearing chunks out of his legs and thighs, and then anywhere else they could. Geoff held his left hand and arm out to protect himself and used his right arm in an attempt to fight them off. Eventually, a ship's boat fished him out, but he was badly hurt.

Back onboard, the Master and Mate worked hard to save his life. They were old-school seafarers who'd been on merchant ships through the Second World War, so they'd seen a lot.

Geoff eventually made it ashore and recovered in hospital, but there wasn't much of his left arm left to repair. He ended up in a hospital that was specialising in the early medical practice of plastic surgery and was befriended by foundation members of 'The Guinea Pig Club', a group made up of fighter pilots and bomber aircrew who had undergone plastic surgery for terrible injuries sustained during the Second World War. These men, usually with the most frightening facial damage, looked after Geoff like a son, and he owed his extensive physical and mental recovery to their great care and friendships.

He was there for nearly a year before he went back to sea, and that's when the adventures really started! I can't tell you much about these years, except to say that by the time I'd met him, Geoff had been everywhere and done everything. Some of our fellow seamen suggested that Geoff would have had to be 150 years old to have fit in all his claimed adventures, but even if it was all bullshit, they were still good stories.

Out on the oilfields a better mentor could not be had. When Geoff realised that I was keen, and had some feel for the job, he taught me everything he knew: techniques and methods that have carried me through my long career as a competent Master, ship handler and marine pilot.

At one point Geoff brought his three sons to meet us, all younger versions of their dad and a very dangerous-looking bunch. In time Geoff found himself a new woman, a very large, pink, round German woman with a heavy accent. Surprisingly, she had three daughters that all looked like smaller versions of her. I think you can see where this is heading. Geoff told me one morning that he was a bit concerned about his household: now that they were all living in one big house, the three piratical sons had each jumped aboard a large pink *Fräulien*, and the house was in chaos.

Time marched on, and Geoff told us that he was going to swallow the anchor. He'd often rattled on about some story involving gold that had been buried by the wife's family during the Second World War. His plan was to dig it up and live happily ever after. No one paid too much attention.

But Geoff never came back, and we never saw, nor heard, from him again – he just disappeared. Many years later one of the engineers went on a Rhine River cruise and went for a walk along the quay one day. Berthed alongside was a beautiful Rhine barge, associated with the idyllic lifestyle of a select and wealthy few. And there, with his feet up, with coffee and a big cigar, was Geoff! He'd found the gold after all (although the original source of it was never talked about).

KIPPER THE WELL-FED DOG

It was quite a change when a qualified cook walked up the gangway to our ASHV for the first time – a very welcome change in some cases! But the cooks, of course, came from working on bigger ships, and some had difficulty in adjusting to the smaller spaces and violent motion. It's a great way to eat less, sitting in the messroom listening to the seasick cook spewing his guts out into the galley bin as he cooks your dinner! Biscuits and cheese will do just fine, thanks.

The cooks also brought with them the requirements and standards expected of their profession; in some cases, standards that their respective unions had fought long and hard for. Food stores and provisions were never a problem, as the oil companies took pride in providing the very best quality food, and quantities were never questioned, as food and victualling costs were minimal compared to other operating costs and big-money revenue. But one of the peculiarities was that, while a cook would always prepare several choices for lunch, he additionally had to always have a roast available for anyone who wanted one. Generally, everyone was well satisfied with a smaller lunch, and day after day the beautifully prepared roast beef, lamb or pork, together with all the trimmings, would go untouched. There may have been a little bit kept for cold cuts, but usually the whole lot would be pulled straight out of the oven and dumped in the Rosie.

With up to six ships in port at any one time, the amount of food dumped was staggering.

We had a manager ashore, a port captain, who looked after the day-to-day requirements of the hard-working ships and crews. As well as general maintenance and survey requirements, there was always gear to be replaced and repaired; main engines and ancillaries needing attention; electronic issues; fuel to be delivered and loaded; garbage to be disposed of; food stores to be arranged and loaded; drilling commodities and cargo to be loaded; crews leaving and joining; accidents and incidents – endless requests of every description, all to be done on the one day so the ship could quickly be turned around and get back to making money ASAP.

The port captain had a ute, and during the working day (and night) it could always be found parked at the bottom of a gangway while he raced aboard to fix a fuck-up of some sort. He and his wife lived locally (not that he ever got home very much!) and had a nice dog, a sort of Labrador-cross called Kipper. One day, as the port captain was racing down a gangway, he came across a cook lugging the garbage bags full of food ashore and asked if he could take home a little of the leftover meat as a treat for Kipper.

'No problem,' said the cook, and a monstrous serve of beef Wellington was thrown in the back of the ute.

Inside of the week, the word had quickly spread around all of the ships and their cooks that poor Kipper was starving to death and desperately needed meat – preferably roasted and with all the trimmings. By noon a few days later, the port captain's ute was 'full and down', generously piled high with bags and bags of the finest roast meats available – and each successive day was the same!

So as not offend anyone, the port captain stored the bags in his garage, but the cooks took this as a sign that poor Kipper was still hungry, and generously supplied more!

Eventually common sense kicked in and an alternative was found at the local nursing home, which enthusiastically accepted the fine foods.

Kipper was saved!

A ROTTEN SHIP

The penalty for drinking on an OSV is understood by everyone: instant dismissal. It's very dangerous work using big, heavy gear – 75–100 millimetre wires and shackles that need two men to carry them – all in heavy weather with a low freeboard that gets plenty of water on deck. They also have small crews, which means that you need full confidence in your crewmates' abilities.

But there is always someone who will fuck it up. In more than 15 years in the offshore oil industry, I had only seen it happen once, and that was bad enough. But there was one ship that took it to another level. Word got back to the Company that one of the ships was rotten, from top to bottom. The Master had allowed grog onboard, and he was part of the drinking sessions being held on the bridge, sometimes while tied up stern-first to a rig. Someone on the rig had reported it – rightfully, as their lives could also be compromised by drunks. The Company moved swiftly, and I found myself on a plane at short notice with clear instructions to 'fix it'.

I found the ship alongside in a shitty North West Shelf port. The gangway was filthy and unattended. There was no one around, no sign of any activity at all, and a dirty, tattered Australian ensign hung limply. The flag is always a good measure of what you will find onboard. A hard-working ship will inevitably look shitty, as there isn't the luxury of time to carry out maintenance and painting, but there is always time to fly a clean and tidy flag, a sign of pride and professionalism.

I walked aboard and copped a good greasy streak on my clean jeans, and the rusty, neglected tow wire immediately caught my eye, together with tools, rags and rubbish laying around all over the place. A towing ship's whole functionality revolves around this very expensive piece of equipment, so no matter what state the rest of the ship is in, the tow wire should be properly stowed, oiled and covered, ready for action at all times. It is the heart and soul of a towing vessel – it earns the money, and it will kill you if it breaks. A professional and experienced offshore sailor can tell in 30 seconds what sort of ship they are looking at, and this one failed on every account.

The previous Master had already 'gone up in the basket' – got the sack. The expression comes from immediate dismissal while at sea, when the sacked person goes up onto the oil rig via the personnel basket on the crane, thence ashore via helicopter – never to return. (And they'd have to find their own way home, too!)

Stepping into the accommodation, it was the same message: total neglect. Filthy alleyways, greasy pawprints on the bulkheads and doors, the pissy smell from uncleaned toilets – fucking awful! In the messroom, the picture was the same, including the sullen, scruffy crew lounging around with their boots on the table.

'You know who I am. Get your fucking boots off the table,' I barked. 'Get a watchman out on deck and clean down the gangway; I don't like getting covered in shit when I come onboard.'

Nothing. Zero response. Great start.

I found something to eat and sat down at the table when one of the tough guys pulled up a seat opposite and leaned across for the big stare-down. I'd been in the game a long time by then. I'd seen the good and the bad, and some things these guys had never even imagined. So I really didn't give a fuck about this sort of tactic.

As I chewed away, I noticed he had a big angry scab above his right eyebrow, so I focused on inspecting that. My staring made him conscious of the scab, and when he gave it a rub there came a big fucking surprise for both of us. WTF! The scab cracked and a shitload of maggots squirted out and dropped on the table. I was, admittedly, a bit taken aback, but the tough guy lost his shit. It was a great moment, and very satisfying to see him falling over the chairs as he made a hasty exit.

It turned out he'd banged his head on some steel casing while coming back from the pub. With lots of flies around – dirty, untidy fucker that he was – guess what was going to happen?

Within weeks I'd got rid of most of the crew and replaced them with decent, hard-working seafarers who appreciated the job. Within a month she looked like every other of the Company's ships – cleaned down inside and out, tidy, businesslike and happy. The immaculate galley and messroom rang with music and conversation, and lunch smelled pretty damned good. The tow winch and freshly greased tow wire gleamed, and the nice clean flags were all flying in the correct places.

Too easy!

FLIPPER

A very heavy piece of towing equipment hit the deck with a thud, but the sound was slightly muffled by a sailor's foot being squashed underneath it. His mates yanked him out and got him to the messroom; I hauled the ship off to a safe position away from the drillship and rushed down to see the damage. What a mess.

The sailor was wearing steel-capped work boots, as was the requirement, but the steel toe-cap had collapsed under the enormous weight and guillotined his toes off. He was in enormous pain, and shock was setting in. I gave him strong painkillers, and while they were taking effect we sawed away with everything we had to remove the heavy work boot and sock. The steel toe-cap fell on the deck with a ghastly mess of toes trapped inside.

Trauma surgeons and battle-hardened paramedics can probably take this in their stride, but my mental preparation when confronted with this level of blood and guts was zero. I had to invent it as I went.

An engineer rushed off with the toe-cap to the engine

room workshop, and I was left to quell the bleeding and stitch a flap up over the bloody mess; only the sailor's little toe remained connected. The engineers couldn't open up the steel toe-cap and extract the four toes, which was just as well for me because I had no fucking idea what I was going to do with them anyway. We made our patient as comfortable as we could while awaiting a medevac helicopter to turn up.

With a clatter and a roar, the chopper appeared over our work deck. It was back to the controls for me to manoeuvre the ship into the best position so the helicopter could winch down a paramedic and stretcher. I felt a lot better doing what I do best, rather than pretending to be a medico!

One of my crew went out to meet the paramedic armed with a broom. As the helicopter winched him down closer to the deck, the paramedic grabbed hold of the offered broom to steady himself – the static electric charge from a helicopter winch cable can deliver quite a kick!

The paramedic had a quick look and was well pleased with my efforts; he hit the patient harder with some painkilling drugs and strapped him into the stretcher. All hands got the stretcher out on deck, and within minutes the patient was winched up and on his way to hospital.

It's always an awful time just after an accident – blood and gore all over the place and everyone deep in thought, realising that it could have been them and wondering what might have been done to prevent such a thing. But it was back to work;

the job has to go on. The workload for the deck crew was now a lot higher with one man short. My workload had increased, too, and the thought of all the paperwork and reports I would have to churn out was giving me a headache!

Several months later, the sailor returned to my ship, minus his toes but with a medical certificate saying he was fit to work again. It turned out that his little toe was just enough to provide the feedback needed to walk without a limp and move properly. He was a great bloke and a first-class seaman, and it was great to have him and his funny-looking foot back in the ship, where he quickly scored the nickname 'Flipper'.

Every Christmas we would put up a small tree in the messroom, nicely decorated and with a few small presents for all onboard. Flipper always got the same present: a brand new pair of thongs!

AN OVERSUPPLY OF GROG

Ship's Masters come in many shapes and forms, and with different levels of certification and experience. The offshore oil industry was unique in that the key criterion was that you could drive a ship – figure out the certification levels later. Some ships you sail, others you command, rig boats you drive!

Driving a ship requires great skill. It's hard to learn and even harder to teach; you're either good at it or find another job. These ships are by necessity small, but very powerful and agile. They operate in very confined spaces, close to multi-million dollar structures such as drilling rigs, production platforms and construction barges, and in very heavy weather – such as Bass Strait or the North Sea.

The Master drives them – hands-on. There were two big levers (port and starboard main engines/propellers), another lever to operate the bow thruster (bow propeller), and a small tiller to move the two rudders. By using a combination of all these levers, the Master could do anything.

In the boom times offshore, big companies would charter ships from all over the world, anything they could get their hands on, and then deliver the ships back to their owners on completion of the job. Sometimes the Company would put a Master on a chartered ship relaxed in the knowledge that he was a good driver and a good operator. But if his Certificate of Competency (CoC) was a coastal one, not an international one, another Master with a Foreign-Going ticket would have to be called in to return the ship.

Bill was a great mate of mine, a gifted driver and very experienced in the offshore game, but he only had a Coastal CoC. So when it came time to deliver the ship back to Singapore, I was called in to help. I flew across to Geraldton and joined the ship: a nice, new German one. It was great to catch up with Bill, and he was happy for me to be there. He'd moved out of his Captain's cabin for me, which was unnecessary, but a nice gesture.

In those days, when delivering ships on an ocean passage, the companies relaxed the total ban on alcohol, so these journeys were great fun; more like a cruise.

As the new Master, I had to prepare all the documentation before we set off. It was around 10am and I suggested that Bill grab some cash out of the Master's safe and buy some grog for the trip. We had ten men and seven days so ... ten cases of beer, 12 bottles of wine and a bottle of scotch should do it.

Thirty minutes before sailing at 1800 (6pm), I went to the bridge and did the pre-departure checks with the Second Mate. All good: the huge main engines were running and there was a nice burble coming from the twin funnels. The crew was standing by the gangway and mooring ropes, the harbour pilot was onboard, I had the port clearance in my hand, and the agent and customs officials were standing on the wharf. Ready to go. But wait: 'Where the fuck is Bill?' I yelled to the Mate, who just shrugged.

Finally, there was a loud screech of tyres as a small delivery van from 'Geraldton Licensed Grocers' skidded around the corner on two wheels and pulled up at the gangway. Both doors opened and out tumbled Bill, together with his new best mate the grocer, both rotten pissed and very, very loud.

'Sort that lot out will you, ASAP!' I told the Mate on the handheld.

The crew reefed Bill aboard, after much hugging and pledging of eternal friendship with the grocer, and shoved him in a cabin. The grocer flung open the side doors of the van and it was 'full and down': chock-a-block with cases of wine and spirits, and boxes and boxes of beer. Enough for 40 men for two months. But we were ten men for seven days! WTF.

All hands pitched in and the boxes and cartons were transferred onboard under the baleful gaze of the customs officers and agent, whose reaction was more personal than professional – all the grog had been bought at full shore retail prices, not duty-free.

'Let everything go, fore and aft,' I yelled. 'Let's get the fuck out of here.'

Away we went, out past the breakwater and into the Indian Ocean – next stop Tuas, Singapore. The next morning a very sick and sad looking Bill came to the bridge.

'Got a bit carried away,' he said.

'The safe's empty,' I said. 'How much was in there?'

'Twelve hundred dollars,' he said, unable to look me in the eye.

Now I had a big problem. Once we handed the ship back to the owners, everything onboard was theirs. I would have to recover the money by selling the grog to the ship's staff while on passage, because it was obvious that no one in their right mind would buy the stuff in Singapore at Australian prices. I was well and truly fucked.

All onboard knew what had happened. I had to start moving this stuff, quickly. I said to the IR (integrated rating) on the 8 to 12 watch, 'You can knock off at ten if you buy a slab of beer.'

'Done,' he said. And to be fair, everyone tried their best, but every time I looked in the spare cabin, the mountain of grog barely seemed to have been touched. I needed another plan.

'Tell the chief Engineer to come and see me, please,' I said on the blower to the engine room.

He appeared.

'Chief, I need an engine breakdown,' I said.

'No way,' he said. 'We've worked our arses off to keep the engines in tip-top condition, there's no way anything is going to break down!'

'Pleeease!' I implored.

The next morning the big main engines went quiet and the ship rolled to a stop in a gentle swell, hundreds of miles away from anything and anywhere. The barbecue flashed up, and out rolled the grog. By 3pm everyone was toast, and couldn't fit another beer in.

'How about a scotch, rum, vodka or gin?' I suggested.

We had two more breakdowns and logged some freakishly localised bad weather and strong currents to try and drag the voyage out for as long as possible. By now everyone onboard was suffering and many took the pledge to never drink again!

Then karma kicked in. Bill was on watch as we were passing through Sunda Straits with a lot of thunderstorm activity around us. As I left the bridge, making my way down the stairway, there was a massive explosion. I rushed back up the stairs and found Bill laying on the bridge wing deck – what a sight! My ship had been hit by lightning and the bolt had struck the mast truck, zapped down to the monkey island and flashed across the bridge wing. Fortunately, it hadn't struck Bill, but it did blow his glasses off and caused his thick, curly black hair and beard to stick straight out, which was a pretty bizarre sight! The massive explosion had deafened him, and it took a couple of days for his hearing to be restored. The extra couple of bottles of Scotch I offloaded onto his account while he was still stunned helped me, too!

We made it to Singapore and slipped alongside at Tuas. I made sure everyone bought a few bottles of what was left – some to take home and some to use in the hotel, plus a bracket of beer cans for the bus ride to the hotel and airport. It was hard work, but I eventually got rid of most of the grog. I managed to offload the few remaining cases of Australian beer to the German Master – more of a curiosity item to him than a valued purchase, really.

GETTING HITCHED

We had a good idea of what we wanted our wedding to be like: lots and lots of friends, a simple civil ceremony in a garden, easy food, plenty of grog and good music – and also we had to somehow include our relatives.

Things fell into place pretty easily. My wife-to-be, Sandy, had access to a beautiful trust mansion nearby, which was available for hire. We had a friend who had a mobile music/light show, and we'd also befriended a lesbian couple who had a nice fondue restaurant and were keen to help. Plans were planned, bookings made, and invitations posted – so far, so good. Sandy spelled out to me very, very clearly that total sobriety was the order of the day – at no stage of the proceedings was I allowed to be swayed by my piss-pot mates.

Right; fully understood, no problem ...

The big day arrived and the best men (two of 'em) and myself got rigged up: matching blue suits with fashionable big lapels and flared trousers; open-neck shirts and hairy chests; clogs and long hair – very cool. We went to the public bar of the Beaumaris Hotel and had a couple of very small beers before all climbing onto the bench seat of the F100 pick-up truck – classy.

At the venue, we assumed our positions in the magnificent garden contained by the driveway, and people started to trickle in; everything was looking good, even the weather. The crowd slowly swelled, dominated by a core of hard-faced relatives of the bride, who had never liked me from the start. But there was no sign of the bride and her sister.

Time dragged on, and on. People were soon getting restless, and the few beers were taking effect; I badly needed a piss.

Finally, and to the great relief of all, a flash hire car swung in through the gates and glided up the horseshoe driveway. The best man took one look at the passengers of the car and gave me an alarmed nudge. 'They're brunettes, both of 'em!' Last time I'd checked both my wife-to-be and her sister were very definitely blonde. WTF! The best man ambled over to speak to the driver and came back with the news: 'Wrong bride – wrong address! Hire car company fucked up.'

I was really busting for a piss now. 'I don't care who it is,' I told him. 'Pull her out of the car and I'll marry her anyway!'

But the driver got it sorted (no mean feat before the invention of mobile phones), and the car moved off and disappeared out the gate. Assuming that the bride had woken up to herself at the last minute, the hostile relatives made for the gate, too.

This was becoming stressful. Now I needed a piss, *and* a drink.

Finally another car swung into the driveway and was clearly carrying fully rigged blondes – thank fuck for that! They pulled up, the door swung open and out tumbled my wife-to-be and sister, both obviously totally pissed and very, very loud.

(It was revealed later that Sandy's cat had hidden under the house and wouldn't come out, and they had glugged a full bottle of scotch between them while solving this problem!)

The hostile relatives begrudgingly returned as my wife-to-be and sister made it into the garden, noisily tripping over themselves as their shoes fell off, and finally the ceremony could commence. Somehow we stumbled our way through the slurred ceremony and the dirty deed was done. The next step was to make our way into the mansion, through the elaborate entrance hall and into the ballroom.

As expected, all hell broke loose as our raucous friends found the bar and the music started to crank up. The bitter, stony-faced relatives found their way to tables, staring glumly at the fondue pots and accoutrements, all a total mystery to most of them. My new father-in-law disappeared to the kitchen to check that our friends had everything under control and ready to go – not quite so ... Under the pressure of their very first wedding dinner, the couple had got into a big blue and were now wrestling and strangling each other on the galley floor, slithering and sliding amongst the recently thrown fondue ingredients and breadsticks. Eventually they were pulled apart, panting and cursing, and the ingredients for lunch were scraped off their clothes and the galley deck. A quick check for boot prints and foreign bodies, and everything was scooped up and back into the pot in record time – problem solved.

We hoped that the scalding hot oil had killed off all of the bacteria picked up from the galley floor, and the cheese chocolate fondues were a huge success – chocolate-covered missiles flying around the room were testimony to that! We struggled through a few speeches, complicated by the drunken bride's inability to string two words together, and then the festivities really started. With the music blaring and our wild friends spasmodically leaping and jumping, the relatives populating the surrounding chairs stared in disbelief. Their disbelief turned to horror – an emotion I shared with them – when it became clear our DJ friend had introduced hardcore porn images to his light show, which were now moving slowly across the walls and ceiling. Some aunties were horrified, most were seriously confused, and some looked smugly pleased!

The new bride got a second lease on life and called for the Scotch; by this point her beautiful (hired) wedding gown was battle-scarred with grass stains, chocolate, cheese and wines of every colour – I gave up on my promise of sobriety and joined the yard-glass drinking squad.

Eventually, traditionally, it was time for my new wife and I to depart, and we crawled out to the waiting car with everyone following along screaming good wishes, and other more clinical advice.

I realised pretty quickly that the driver was pissed when we took off leaving a big skid mark on the manicured driveway and sideswiped the ornate gate. As we blasted out through the gate, the driver yelled out something to the effect that the party was far too good to leave. So we did a quick U-turn into the other gateway, sped up the driveway and stopped just before running over our guests.

A great cheer went up, the driver fell out the door, and we all rushed back in – the party cranked up again. The terrified family and relatives used the diversion to scuttle out the door, helping themselves to the presents on the way out.

HONEYMOON CRUISE

Early in the morning after our wedding, when the bride and her cat finally crawled out from underneath a huge pile of gift-wrapping paper, it was a mad panic to get cleaned up and on our way to the airport for our honeymoon in Tahiti.

Somehow we got onboard our flight and, via Auckland, eventually made it to Faaa Airport, Papeete. By this time it was very early in the morning, and zombie-like we made it onto a bus destined for the port and thence an hour ferryboat ride across to the island of Moorea.

Hungover, tired, dirty and fed up, we hung on for grim death as the bus thundered down the dirt road. On arrival at the port, the bus driver threw our bags in a heap and roared off. Nothing was open, and this shitty part of the port was deserted except for a run-down inter-island ferry laying alongside the wharf – quite literally, as it had a 10-degree list to starboard and looked to me like the only thing keeping it upright were the mooring lines.

The ferry seemed to be loaded with various animals, so the starboard list turned out to be quite fortunate, allowing the piss and dung to flow overboard into the harbour. We waited and waited, and there was no sign of anyone at all, and definitely no sign of the luxury launch we'd been promised. I found a vending machine and bought two bottles of warm beer – breakfast. My beautiful wife was now looking a bit battle-worn, and was getting nasty; the warm beer wasn't welcome, apparently.

Out of the blue, a grubby, unshaven Frenchman appeared, mumbled something and stumbled off towards the crappy-looking ferry.

Following along behind him, dragging our suitcases, it finally dawned on us that this was our luxury launch. We paddled onboard through the accumulated dung and piss, past the penned-up pigs, goats, and chickens, and found our way upstairs to a grubby, run-down passenger area furnished with an array of broken plastic chairs. I snarled and wrestled a couple of chairs for us near a window – but by now the red mist was descending; I'd had enough.

As a professional seafarer and ship's Master I was interested to observe preparations and the vessel's readiness for sea; it didn't take long – there weren't any. All of a sudden the engines were started, and without any warm-up or checks they immediately went to full ahead just in time for the ratty mooring ropes to be let go from the wharf, still trailing perilously close to the now-thrashing propellers.

At last we were on our way; the final leg. I hoped a nice cruise across to the island might perk us up a bit.

Certainly did; everyone perked up. As the rusty piece of shit cleared the breakwater it hogged into a big ocean swell and buried the bows with a great shudder. The stern lifted the propellers out of the water flow and the engines over-sped and made a horrible sound. Then the bows went skyward again, the rudder went hard over and we span around onto our heading. This, of course, put the swell on the beam, and then rolling started.

By the feel of things she was very 'tender' with minimal stability, and it seemed we were very close to rolling right over. Probably next to no fuel or ballast in the double-bottom tanks, a high profile and high wind heel factor – a deadly combination. Each successive roll was deeper, and the roll rate to return upright seemed to take longer each time. Going by the appearance of the ship and staff I was quite sure that stability calculations and criteria hadn't been high on the list of pre-departure checks and procedures.

The screams from the captive pigs and goats did little to ease my concern, and the passengers, including my now very fragile wife, simultaneously dived for the windward windows. The animal screams from down below were now muffled by the sound of herd-vomiting; once one or two started, the rest joined in. The windward windows did not help, either.

I was now not feeling too good myself: a monstrous hangover, no food, a couple of warm breakfast beers and the stench of animals and spew were taking their toll.

I made for a window (leeward) and stuck my head out for some fresh air, just as the ferry took a mighty roll.

Splat, right on the back of my head, warm, liquid, and plenty of it. Fuck me, I thought.

Thankfully I quickly realised that it wasn't fresh vomit, but warm entrapped rainwater from the deck above – a near miss nevertheless.

Eventually, somehow, we shuddered our way around a breakwater and smacked alongside a little jetty. A lopsided sign suspiciously stating 'Welcome to Club Mediterranee' greeted us, as did a squad of handsome staff togged up in matching shorts and shirts, and big shit-eating grins.

I wish I could say things improved from there, but they didn't. In the following week, my new wife and I were showered with bugs while we slept in our traditional bure and got food poisoning *and*, in my case, dengue fever. By the time we finally managed to wrestle our passports away from the rodent-like receptionist and cancel the final days of our stay, I couldn't have been happier to see that miserable ferry again.

A REAL-LIFE ADMIRAL

Purpose-built, state-of-the-art, anchor-handling offshore support vessels (OSVs) are very specialised, very expensive and good for nothing except the specific requirements by the offshore oil and gas industry. But occasionally the ships are chartered in by other, unusual, organisations. The Royal Australian Navy, for example.

It's not worth the navy's while to own, operate, and maintain such specialised vessels, so we were called upon to install some very sophisticated mooring systems for the new Collins class submarines based at Garden Island in Western Australia.

No big deal for our ship, but we were to have navy personnel onboard to oversee the task, as well as navy sailors to help with the grunt on deck. The Royal Australian Navy and the 'Merchant Navy' are worlds apart, but interestingly, the real sailors of both institutions have a lot of common ground. The navy sailors that came aboard were great. These were real sailors, not just forklift drivers, truck drivers or storemen – they were proper hands-on 'scaly-backs', and we all hit it off right from the start.

The deck work was hard and heavy going, and the days were long, but an unusual bonus for us was that we tied up every night at the brand new, yet to be commissioned navy base and made very good use of the senior sailors' mess (bar). One morning, I left my cabin and went down a couple of decks to our messroom to grab a coffee. There was a bit of commotion going on, and as I stepped into the doorway, I saw an apparition: a full-blown, fully rigged, Royal Australian Navy Admiral. WTF! He was a very big man, with a fine salt-and-pepper beard, and looked immaculate in sparkling, tailored whites and flash gold braid.

While I was composing myself, one of my IRs who was sitting at the table with the morning paper, yelled, 'Oi! Take ya fucking shoes off. Can't ya read the fucking sign?'

Hard-working rig boats, with work decks covered in greasy winches, wires and shackles, always have a strict 'no boots or work clothes' policy inside the accommodation. The admiral was no exception, but by the look on his face it had been a long time since anyone had spoken to him like that or told him what to do, let alone a scruffy-arsed sailor who then added from behind his newspaper, 'That'll cost ya a slab of beer, too, I reckon.'

His driver, a navy sailor, helped the admiral climb out of the royal shoes. I quickly hustled him, in his socks, up the stairs to the wheelhouse and showed him around. This admiral was also a real sailor at heart and he really enjoyed being onboard a working ship. 'It wouldn't take much to paint this navy grey and fly a white ensign instead of that red ensign!' he said. Eventually, it was time for the admiral to leave. His driver helped him climb aboard the royal shoes and off he went in the Ford LTD with his pennant flying from the bonnet.

The next morning I was standing outside on the bridge wing with a cup of coffee when I spotted the big Ford pull up at our gangway. A sailor jumped out, popped the boot, heaved a slab of beer onto his shoulder and ran up the gangway.

'With the compliments of the admiral,' he said.

THAT'S GOTTA HURT

The big AHSV was making very hard work of it. Deep in the Southern Ocean with 40 knots of wind on the nose, and a very heavy sea and swell, the going was tough – not to mention the 1500 metres of 85-millimetre-thick tow wire and enormous semi-submersible drilling rig being towed behind.

As Master, I watched the bow fall away as a deep trough passed by, subconsciously noting the twin rudders being applied by the autopilot and the clicking of the Master gyro compass as the heading was picked up again. I could feel the main engine governors working as they adjusted to the varying load put on them as the towing ship sat into a different wave trough to the rig, nearly a mile astern.

The bridge door crashed open and deposited the Mate and an AB strapped up in their wet-weather gear and boots, and buoyancy vests. They caught their breath and wedged themselves tightly in a corner of the wheelhouse. 'All's okay with the gear, Cap – tow wire chaffing sleeve is doing its job and we freshened the nip, as usual.'

When towing an oil rig, usually the tow wire is heaved in a few metres every so often to reduce the wear caused by chafe and lessen the chance of it carrying away. We were still only making good about 2 knots over the ground – fucking near going backwards.

This brief conversation was interrupted by a blood-curdling scream from below. 'What the fuck was that? Get down there and take a look, Dave!'

As the Mate made for the stairs, he was pushed aside by a fast-moving chief engineer charging up them. 'What's the problem, Chief?' I asked him. 'Sounds like murder!'

'Far worse than that; the second engineer's jammed his cock in the drawer!'

It seemed he'd been having a shave in his cabin, standing at the washbasin in the bollocky, when the ship took a lurch. He fell against the open drawer – which his cock happened to be hanging in – and the drawer slammed shut.

'That's the mighty scream we heard, I guess,' said Dave.

This was met with thoughtful silence and rearranging by all.

'Yep, took two of us to get the drawer open and release his slug,' said the Chief.

A short time later, the ashen-faced second engineer appeared on the bridge in his overalls. A ring of anxious faces peered down as the injured cock was pulled gingerly out of the overalls.

'Can ya fix it, Cap?' asked the second engineer. 'It looks pretty fucked …'

Sure had to agree with that observation.

'Fuck me! That's gotta hurt!' said one of the observers.

'No doubt about that,' said the person attached to the stricken cock, 'but do something, quick – maybe the end will die or something!'

On most merchant ships, the Master has to perform the role of medic. As the number of persons onboard increases, a dedicated medic and then a doctor have to join the crew, but there are plenty of ships that don't reach that point, so all ship's Masters are required to do medical training over and above that required for a first-aid certificate. The additional training also includes several nights in a hospital casualty department, and some time spent in the morgue peering inside customers.

To prepare the Master for this important role, every ship must carry *The Ship Captain's Medical Guide*, first published in 1868. This is jam-packed with text, illustrations and photos covering nearly every type of medical emergency you could think of. *Nearly* every type. 'Squashed cock' did not appear in the index.

When 'The Book' is no help, the next step is to put a call through to a designated hospital, a service provided to ships at sea. Bracing myself against the violent and irregular motion unique to towing vessels in heavy weather, I got on the satellite phone and was patched through to a duty doctor in one of the major hospitals.

It's usually not a pleasant conversation: an overworked doctor is reluctantly dragged away from his patients to listen to some dickhead ship's Master rattle on about a minor problem.

'Good morning, Captain,' said the doctor. 'If I am to be able to assist you, then please slowly and clearly provide me with details of the patient, an accurate and detailed description of the injury, what first aid has been administered, what drugs have been used, the current status of the patient and any other pertinent details; even the smallest detail may be critically important. And please don't waste my time with profanities and flowery descriptions.'

'Second engineer jammed his cock in the drawer,' I said.

'Fuck me,' said the doctor. 'That's gotta hurt.'

'Thanks for the professional observation, Doctor, but we've established that much ourselves.'

'Well, describe to me what it looks like now, compared to how it appeared before the accident,' said the doctor.

'How the fuck would I know? It's not a requirement to check out people's tackle when they join a ship. But there's no blood, and it's flat in the middle and starting to go blue.'

'Mmmmm. Well, not much can be done, really. You'll have to drop him off in the nearest port,' said the doctor.

'What, Mawson in the Antarctic? that'd be the nearest, I reckon – at least he'd have no problem getting an ice pack!'

'Well, get a helicopter to pick him up then,' said the doctor.

'We'll have to wait a fair while for that,' I said, 'because it's going to take them a while to design, test and manufacture one that can fly this fucking far.'

There was a long pause.

'Give him a couple of Panadol and a cold compress, and tell him not to fiddle with it,' was the professional advice from the superior being.

'Not much chance of that,' I said. 'That's what engineers do 23 hours a day!'

Thank you for fuck all.

We eventually got him ashore off Durban two weeks later, and from what I could see (from a distance), things hadn't improved very much!

Years later I bumped into him in George Street, Sydney, and we went to a nearby bar for a drink. He told me he still had a flat spot and offered to show it to me in the loo. I didn't think that was a good idea in a Sydney bar the day before Mardi Gras, so I told him I'd take his word for it.

BASS STRAIT SHUFFLE

In the boom days of offshore oil and gas in Bass Strait, ships' Masters were frequently called upon by the Company to join oil rigs. While operating in Australian waters, the rig required a fully licensed marine crew; everywhere else in the world, the owners of the rig could, and did, employ anyone that took their fancy. The American owners thought we were an unnecessary add-on, worthless and just another huge cost to bear when operating in Australia. It was a shit job for us, too, in every respect, and nobody liked it.

I drew the short straw and was sent to join this big monster in the Bass Strait Oilfields – at the time one of the biggest hostile environment drilling rigs in the world. When drilling was in progress, we were stationed in an office inside one of the 'legs'. The ballast control room was crammed full of electronics and computers, with a big schematic console showing the hundreds of valves, tanks and pumps required to keep the rig in optimum stability and trim.

The driller had a duplicate set of read-outs, and whenever the rig developed the *slightest* list or change of trim, he was hot on the phone to roast us.

Every hour you had to leave the ballast control room, go out into Bass Strait winter weather and check the load on the eight huge anchor windlasses to ensure the anchor chain tensions were constant, and no anchors were dragging. If an anchor dragged and the rig came off location, even by a small amount, it could really disrupt the drilling – any disruption to drilling upset the driller, and could be a death sentence. On an oil rig, the driller is the 'main man'. He's the one paying the bills and taking the chances, so he can do whatever he likes and say whatever he likes without question. To get on the wrong side of him is fatal in that he will have you 'up in the basket' and on your way ashore within the hour – sacked. He needs to be pampered and have his ego massaged at all times.

Returning from one inspection just after midnight, I ducked back into the ballast control room thoroughly drenched. I stripped off my wet-weather coat and hung it on a cabinet to dry. The cabinet was nothing special and had a speaker grill fitted in the front of it. I'd dried off, made a brew and climbed back into my chair at the control console when suddenly all fucking hell broke loose.

The control console lit up with rows of flashing warning lights, bells and horns sounded and, to my horror, all the different control systems began shutting down! WTF! Then I noticed that there was a shift in trim and heel; the rig's ballast control system was not coping at all, and the rig was starting to tilt!

The phone went into meltdown, and the driller was apo-fucking-plectic shrieking on the PA system in some incomprehensible Louisianan swamp dialect. I gasped with terror, grabbed my wet coat off the cabinet and saw a sign that read 'UPS'.

Uninteruptable Power Supply, I twigged, realising that it wasn't a speaker grill at all – it was a meshed vent for the internal cooling fan, and my wet, heavy coat had starved the UPS of cooling air and caused it to trip, which in turn started shutting down all sorts of ballast control systems.

I snatched my coat and threw it away just before an army of wild-eyed rig electricians burst through the door. After a frantic few minutes, they rebooted the systems and everybody calmed down.

'Did you notice anything with the UPS?' one of them asked.

'Who, me? No, mate, everything was running just fine ...'

THE BODY IN THE FREEZER

We were in the middle of the ocean when one of the engineer officers had a massive heart attack and was discovered in the messroom, face-first in a bowl of soup. A ship's Master gets specialised first-aid training, but a death certificate can only be signed off by a medical practitioner, so in this case a sea burial wasn't an option: the body needed to be kept onboard until we reached port.

Unfortunately, there was zero chance of us being released to go to port. Rig-shifting and anchor-handling is very demanding and dangerous work, especially in wild weather, and it's not uncommon to work around the clock. The huge oil rig was preparing to leave the location, which meant that all 16 of its 20-tonne anchors had to be broken out, retrieved, and then got under tow. With half her anchors up, and only half of them down, the rig was in a precarious position. Anchor-handling supply ships (AHSVs), such as ours were critical at this stage and couldn't be released – no exceptions, no excuses.

In cases like these, you're best off freezing the body. The only freezer space big enough is where the food stores are kept, but once the body's bagged up and frozen down it's generally not a problem; you just need to look the other way whenever you go in there. So after it was determined beyond any doubt that the engineer was gone, he was extracted from the soup and zipped up in a body bag.

Three long, hard, sleepless days later, all of the rig's anchors were broken out and housed and the rig gotten under tow by the other AHSV in attendance. We were now freed up to return to port.

The instructions were very clear: get to port, send the body ashore and get back to the rig ASAP. Drilling rigs are delicate things when under tow and need to be continuously pampered and spoilt by the attendant AHSVs.

So we cut loose and headed back to the nearest port at best speed: four main engines at full power, and trimmed down by the head for less drag. On arrival at the very small port, we made our way to the jetty and went alongside. The local copper turned up, but there was no sign of the undertaker. Apparently he was running late, but we had to get back to the rig ASAP. This straightforward task was displaying all the symptoms of a class-A clusterfuck.

Rig boat Masters are groomed to solve problems on the spot. There's usually no time to involve shore-based managers in any decision-making process – 'just fix it', is their usual response. I discovered there was a local fisherman with some refrigerated shipping containers on-site and negotiated a deal with him (six slabs of beer) to store the body for a few hours until the undertaker arrived.

The copper then announced that perhaps he should look inside the bag and make sure everything looked ok. *Seriously?* I thought. *How could a frozen body ever look okay?!* Anyway, down we go to the ship's freezer and drag out the bag. I could tell in an instant that something wasn't right, but before I could do or say anything, the copper pulled the zip down and let out a mighty expletive. The body's head had snapped off at the neck! (And also, it eventuated, had one arm.)

'Jesus fucking Christ!' was the best the copper could do.

Obviously rolling around in the heavy seas had caused the frozen-hard body to brittle fracture, but to all of us standing around peering in the bag, it looked like an axe-murderer had been running amok. But time was ticking. I put all the bits back in the right places, straightened the body up, and the copper calmed down a bit. But it was still a grim task to get the body on the stretcher and down the gangway.

'Let go, fore and aft' never sounded so good, as we headed back to sea.

MORTAL DANGER

What happens in the general community can also happen in a ship, and tragic deaths are no exception. The problem is, when somebody goes missing at sea it can be very hard to determine whether it was an accident, suicide or perhaps even murder.

Accidental falls into the sea aren't uncommon. At night, the ship is blacked out because the bridge watchkeepers need their night vision – essential to spot and identify approaching ships and boats, especially unlit yachts and fishing boats. There are plenty of obstacles and protrusions to be found on ships' decks, and there are always gaps in safety rails and chains where access must be provided, for example, for life-saving appliances such as boats and rafts. It would be easy to fall through, which is why it's never recommended to walk around the dark decks of a ship at night.

Also, people make mistakes: sometimes a safety chain might not be fastened at the end of a day's maintenance work. It would just take one slip, and the splash and screams would be drowned out by the ship's noise – no one would see you go. If it was a high freeboard with a long way down to the water, there's a good chance your neck would break when you hit the water – probably a blessing. I imagine there would be nothing worse than floating around watching your ship disappear into the darkness. Cold, fatigue, dehydration, sharks and barracuda would do the rest.

But sometimes it's not an accident. Seafarers, just like everyone else, can succumb to what they feel is overwhelming pressure and take their own lives – sometimes by jumping overboard out of sight of their shipmates. But with no body, no evidence and no warning, it can be hard to distinguish from an accident, and usually remains one of those mysteries of the sea.

Over the years, one piece of evidence that I did discover after one of my crew members was lost at sea was the absence of a shackle from the ship's inventory. All shackles, blocks (pulleys), wires and chains are recorded in a log together with their test certificates. No certificate and/or record in the inventory and the item is removed from the ship – no exceptions. So it wasn't that difficult to discover that the shackle was missing. This D-shackle had a working load limit of 35 tonnes, weighed 20 kilograms, and had an inside diameter of about 130 millimetres – conveniently about the size of someone's ankle. You only needed one: 20 kilograms of weight securely fastened would do the job, and you'd never be able to unscrew the shackle pin if you changed your mind halfway down.

Accidents, suicide, sure. But could a missing crew member have been a murder victim?

Of course …

A ship is just a small community, and problems occur. I have been fortunate and never experienced one onboard any ship I have been Master of, but there have been plenty of incidents recorded over the years. Usually it starts as arguments aggravated by drugs or alcohol, gambling debts, racial or ethnic disagreements – anything you can think of really.

A murder onboard a ship at sea creates its own problems, as usually the victim disappears over the side, witnesses are obviously reluctant to come forward, and the ship's Master and officers are not trained in the collection of evidence – nor are they able to act as judge, jury or executioner. Everything has to wait until arrival at the next port, which could be weeks away.

But whether accident or not, if you happen to fall overboard and someone notices, there is hope. All ship's crews are regularly exercised in 'man overboard' drill, and the procedure is tried and tested.

Several things happen simultaneously once someone calls, 'MAN OVERBOARD, STARBOARD SIDE.' Which side is very important because the bridge officer, on hearing the shout, will instantly put the rudders over to the same side, which will cant the ship's stern and thrashing propeller away from the person in the water. Otherwise they might be sucked into the water flow going down the side of the hull and into the giant food processor. Messy.

At the same time, the bridge watchkeepers will release both automatic bridge wing lifebuoys, which are equipped with water-activated lights and smoke canisters; they'll push the emergency MoB button on the GPS and record the position; turn on searchlights; and detail one lookout to stare fixedly at the figure in the water and never, ever take their eyes off them. A person's head bobbing around in a rough sea disappears from sight very quickly, even in broad daylight.

The communication system's DSC (digital selective calling) will transmit an automatic emergency call to everyone in the area. If the ship is near other ship traffic, the international code 'O – Oscar' (Morse code: three long blasts) will be sounded on the ship's whistle to notify everyone. The ship is then put into a Williamson turn – pretty much a large question mark-shaped turn that brings the ship back onto its original course, in reverse.

By this time, the two lifebuoys, with lights and smoke, should be sighted on either bow, and the person in the water should be somewhere further on.

The time taken to execute the Williamson turn is used to advise the engine room that the main engines will need to be used, which is sometimes very difficult to do when the ship is on an ocean passage. At the same time, the emergency boat crew will be preparing to launch a boat, and medical preparations will be made to treat hypothermia, shock and/or trauma.

The system has been tested over time; it works. But there are ways to complicate it.

I was Second Mate on a small passenger ship, on an ocean passage at full sea speed, when a middle-aged male passenger placed his drink down on his lunchtime table, walked outside, then stepped up onto the polished teak rail and jumped. The officers and crew were highly skilled, and the man overboard procedure was conducted flawlessly.

I was the officer in charge of the fast rescue boat, and we slipped the falls and got away from the ship's side in record time.

It was quite lonely watching our ship steam away while it made a Williamson turn; fortunately, the weather was fine, clear and calm.

We found the man quite quickly, and I manoeuvred alongside so my crew could grab him and drag him aboard. But he kept swimming away every time we closed on him, and it was proving difficult to manoeuvre the boat to keep up with him.

Over and over again he would swim away.

By this time, the ship had returned and was stopped in the water awaiting our return. All the passengers were lining the rails, fully rigged with the latest cameras and video gear.

I made yet another approach to our determined swimmer, but this time, when he made a move to escape, I had one of the boat crew bash him on the head with an oar. This stunned him enough for another crewman to snag him with a gaff hook, and we wrestled him into the boat where several crewmen sat on him.

Job done.

Unfortunately, the Master was not so impressed with my technique – which, of course, had been repeatedly photographed and filmed by 500 passengers.

Not all ship suicides involve a quiet leap into the water.

I was piloting a ship manned by Croatians down the reef when I heard a horrible noise outside my cabin window. I raced outside and a man was hanging by his neck from the steel stairway, strangling to death as the electrical cord was pulled tightly by his weight.

It was all very sudden and brutal.

I let out a mighty yell, raced back into my cabin and grabbed my trusty Swiss Army knife. I sawed through the cable and he dropped on the deck, but was still strangling as the electrical cord had pulled tight and the plastic coating had jammed the knot. I had no choice but to dig into the meat of his neck to get the blade under the cord and cut him free.

By this time, several crewmen had turned up, but there wasn't much anyone could do to help until I eventually cut the cord away.

What a mess. Blood everywhere and he'd shat his pants, too. WTF.

The crew took over and lugged him off. The cut I'd made to his neck wasn't too bad and they fixed that up okay, but he'd damaged his voice box and couldn't speak. I went to see him and he was very obviously unhappy to see me, which confused me a bit.

Afterwards, I went to the bridge and the Master called me aside and thanked me for my efforts. He told me that this Croatian engineer had tied the electrical cord around his neck and the other end to the handrail stanchion, then rolled himself through the gap in the railing. Then, alarmingly, he explained that this was actually a repeat occurrence, and that the engineer had tried on two other occasions to neck himself as he'd just been notified that his entire family, wife and several young children had been killed in the war back home.

It was very sad, and depressed me immensely.

Attempted or threatened suicides are not uncommon, and quickly become a pain in the arse. Of course, they clearly indicate a very troubled person, but I find these threats are often empty – if they were serious, then there were always plenty of 35-tonne shackles around. Regardless, the issue always has to be addressed and it's usually time-consuming, and always involves a lot of paperwork for the Master. Just go away and make your threats somewhere else!

The last one I had was on a nice modern OSV. I got a call at night by the bridge officer on anchor watch to say that a crewman was threatening to suicide because of problems at home.

I went to the bridge and was met by the Bosun (the leading seaman), who explained that this young guy was threatening to top himself, but that they had arranged for another crewman to be with him at all times through the night. Hopefully we could get a launch out in the morning and get him ashore.

The matter was pretty much contained and managed onboard. The man had problems at home, so if we could get him ashore and home with the minimum of fuss, the ship would have no further part in the matter.

Easy?

No, it's never easy.

I returned to my bunk and thought no more of the matter, until my satellite phone awoke me. It was a very senior police officer calling to tell me that police had received a frantic call from one of my crew members, who was about to carry out a very bloodied suicide.

Now, of course, the fairly simple matter has elevated itself to a higher level.

The Bosun and I had a talk with the guy, and he looked sheepish when I told him that the police were involved. It seemed that he had secretly made the call to the local police and sort-of forgot to mention it.

I pointed out to him that it was now a big deal, and he had created a raft of problems for himself – not the least that the police would probably not allow him to board a commercial flight home. He hadn't thought this out too well, it now appeared. He also surprised me by saying that he'd done this very same thing on two previous ships that he'd worked on and that, in his opinion, as Master I had not received sufficient training to be able to cope with people such as him. WTF.

I pointed out to him that maybe a life at sea was not his calling, and perhaps he should fuck off and get a job in Kmart?

I couldn't get rid of him quickly enough. At first light, I managed to arrange a launch from ashore, and the police had advised that they would be there to meet him.

As the launch approached, I told the Mate to go down and supervise the operation. He looked a bit surprised when I told him to make sure he stood close behind the seaman at the head of the short ladder, and give him a helpful foot in the back when he hesitated on the way down to the launch.

They always do this – having second thoughts, I guess?

The boat headed off and the Mate returned to the bridge with a smile on his face.

'Exactly as you said!' He reported

Experience pays.

STARSKY AND HUTCH

Ships' Masters in any ports are usually treated well by police officers when it comes to incidents onboard. They never hesitate to promptly attend a vessel and are always very supportive of the Master. Over the years I have made some good friends in the force, and never hesitate to look them up if I'm around.

Once while in a small port there was a theft onboard my ship. My safe had been opened after I'd left my keys on my desk, and about $1000 cash had been taken along with some serious painkillers that we carry in case of medical emergencies. It was obviously someone onboard, so my port manager arranged for the local detectives to come and have a look around.

The two detectives were a couple of crusty old guys, clearly well seasoned. In a very short time, they interviewed everyone onboard and reported to me who they thought the culprit was. No hard evidence, just a policeman's sixth sense. They suggested that if they 'leaned on this person a bit' we'd have an answer pretty quick. With my approval, they did, and they

152

were right. Problem solved. We had a few coffees and a good yabber before Starsky and Hutch went on their way.

We worked out of that port on and off for a year and the pair regularly dropped by. One time we were stuck in port with serious engine control problems and a computer technician from the manufacturer was sent down to fix it. One of our engineers, Marcus, asked to borrow the technician's hire car to go to the pub. The technician was reluctant because another driver wouldn't be covered by insurance, but Marcus was on a mission and eventually got his way.

On the way to the pub, sober, Marcus spun the hire car into a ditch and virtually wrote it off. The technician was upset, to say the least.

The next morning, Starsky and Hutch happened to drop in for a coffee and a yarn. I told them about Marcus pranging the car, and they offered to wind him up. I rang the Engine Control Room and summoned Marcus to my cabin to be interviewed by the police, and a very meek version of him soon appeared at the door.

'Take a seat, Marcus, and tell us what happened,' said Starsky.

'Well,' said Marcus, 'I came around a bend and there was a cow in the middle of the road. I swerved to miss it and ran off the road into the culvert and rolled the car.'

'Very common down here, being a big dairy farm area,' Starsky said. 'What colour was the cow?'

I could see Marcus pink up as he blurted out, 'It was brown, a brown cow.'

'You sure it was brown? Dark brown, reddish brown?'

'More a reddish, darkish brown,' stammered Marcus.

'Ah,' said Starsky.

'That's where we have a problem,' said Hutch, who had previously been keeping quiet. 'You see, down here all of the dairy cows are Friesians, and Friesians are black and white. The brown cow you saw is a brown Swiss, a very expensive show animal only recently imported from Europe. Any of the locals would have known this and taken care to ensure it was safe and sound. This cow you nearly hit subsequently ran through a wire fence, causing serious injury, and had to then be put down by a vet. The farmer is furious and demanding compensation.'

Marcus looked unwell. He began sweating heavily, shifting in his seat.

'So, you'd better get changed and we'll go and have talk with the farmer,' Hutch said. 'Get moving!'

Marcus raced off and came back in jeans and a T-shirt.

'No, go and put a proper collared shirt on, a blue one. Farmers like blue shirts,' said Starsky.

Off Marcus raced again.

The two detectives kept Marcus wriggling for a while, and I had to step outside to hide my laughter. When I returned, Starsky stood up to face the now terrified engineer and said, 'Fuck off, Marcus, you're a dickhead!' We all cracked up.

A long time later, I came across one of the detectives again in very different circumstances. I was lecturing Master 4 at SEAMEC (South East Australia Maritime Education Centre), at Lakes Entrance in Victoria. I discovered that I enjoyed the challenge of teaching, that I had the knowledge and experience the students were hungry for, and I was pretty good at it. You certainly wouldn't do it for the money. Anyway, they put me up in accommodation nearby for the duration of each course.

One night I woke to find someone silently standing by my bed. In the darkness I could only see an outline of his shape, and at first I thought it was the Grim Reaper come to collect me, but then I realised it was someone in a hoodie. I kept very still and quiet while taking this in. The person never moved.

Then I let out a mighty yell, leaped out of bed and lunged after him. He was quick and raced for the door, but I was in hot pursuit when I banged my forehead on a cupboard and landed on my arse.

It was no big deal – nothing was taken – so I locked the door and went back to sleep. In the morning I was surprised to see police officers everywhere: up and down the driveway and out in the street. I opened up the back door and was delighted to see my mate Starsky in his ill-fitting suit.

'Cat burglar,' he said once I'd invited him in for a coffee. 'Some arsehole creeping around and pinching stuff. Knocked over a lot of elderly people in the street. Took their jewellery and stuff. Very sad as it's not expensive stuff but it means a lot to the older folk.'

'He was in here last night,' I said, and described what happened.

Did he hit you? No, I explained, I did that myself.

'Tell me,' he said, looking around my room, 'do you wear pyjamas?'

'No, but what has that got to do with anything?' I said.

'Well, he'll probably file a complaint. Most likely he's seriously traumatised after being chased down by a fat, hairy, naked man screaming his head off.'

We had a good laugh. 'Will you catch him?' I asked

'Probably not,' he replied. 'But you know, it doesn't really matter whether we catch him or not. You see, people like this have a shit-awful life. They don't live like you and me surrounded by nice people, enjoying life and friendships, and making the best of what they've got. They live in a community of shitty people like themselves, always looking over their shoulder, and always in constant fear of being caught. So, it doesn't matter much if we catch them or not; they're already serving a sentence.'

Wise words.

LET THE RECORDS SHOW

Oil rigs are eye-wateringly expensive pieces of machinery, especially new ones, and I have had two sink on me while under tow.

The first one was brand spanking new, straight out of the shipyard in Japan and destined for its first job off the coast of Sakhalin (in the USSR, in those days). We made our way from Singapore up to Japan to pair-tow it to its new home. 'Pair-towing' is when two ocean tugs tow side by side on separate tow wires; 'tandem towing' is one behind the other. It seemed like a straightforward job: jack-ups are easy to tow compared to the big semi-submersibles.

We tied up at a little port in the Inland Sea, together with the other ship, and waited for the rig to be prepared. The other ship engaged to tow had a British Master and officers, and we hit it off well. On their way out from the UK, they'd stopped over in Dubai and someone had acquired an enormous, life-sized toy Pink Panther, which was included in the socialising.

When we towed the brand new rig out of the shipyard everyone turned out to bid farewell in quite a send-off. It was due to start a very lucrative and long charter, and everyone was out to make a good impression. The two powerful OSVs made easy work of the tow through the Inland Sea and out past Osaka, then down Osaka Bay to the open sea.

All OSVs have duplicate controls, forward and aft. Most of the 'driving' is done from the aft controls, and on some ships the control levers are slaved, which means that when you move a lever at one end, the other one moves, too. The Pink Panther's paws had been cable-tied to the forward control levers, and it was funny to see him sitting in the big chair and working away there during the voyage.

But then it all turned to shit when a fierce storm hit just as we cleared the entrance. Some of the gear was carried away, and a 100-millimetre wire got sucked into our starboard propeller. Another port tug came out to help, but to no avail. The rig went aground on the rocky coastline and the rig crew abandoned her by helicopter. Both OSVs cut away their towing gear, and that was that.

However, because this dramatic-looking incident occurred close to shore, the Japanese TV news helicopters made sure they covered every detail. Unfortunately, this also included footage of the Pink Panther working away feverishly at the controls. It must have been very confusing for the viewers, not to mention the owner of the rig, but they might have thought it explained how the incident happened!

The lawyers were on to that one like sharks on a whale

carcass. (After several years, it was determined that the towing arrangements were inadequate for the task and the owners should have thought it out better. No blame was ever apportioned to either ship.)

In the meantime, I was put up in a small hotel back in town while things were sorted out. After a quick wash and change of clothes, I was off to the pub. I was about halfway down when the elevator stopped, doors opened, and into the lift stepped my old man. It was a big surprise, to both of us, I guess, but he steadfastly looked ahead, as did I. Not a word was spoken. The doors opened, he went one way, and I went the other, and I never saw him again.

I found out later he'd been appointed to assess the practicalities of salvaging the rig, which it would have looked like I was partly responsible for – kind of ironic, and typical for our relationship, I guess.

Several years later, while pair-towing another rig, this time from Darwin down the West Australian Coast to Fremantle, the rig rolled over backwards and sank. Another frenzy for the lawyers, and it was hardly a surprise when I started getting invited to their Christmas piss-ups!

I left the offshore oil industry for a while and drove a ro-ro back and forth across Bass Strait for a few years. Roll-on/roll-off ships were designed for wheeled cargo, allowing them to drive right on and off at port. They worked hard, with quick turnarounds to keep the dollars flowing. Scores of semitrailers and containers on trailers were driven on via a stern ramp, both underneath, into a cavernous vehicle deck, and also up onto the top weather deck.

It was common for livestock – cattle and sheep – to be transported back and forth in standard road transport trailers. These semitrailers had a portable deck fitted so that two levels of cows could be carried in the one trailer. We had a very rough crossing one night, losing three semitrailers over the side, with a lot more damaged and smashed up both above and below deck. Unfortunately, one of the livestock trailers had wracked due to the ship's rolling, and the portable decking had collapsed. All the livestock fell down into those below, and it was a mad tangle of dead and dying animals and steel decking.

There was nothing we could do. The trailers were parked close together with not even a metre walkway between them, and some of the huge container trailers had toppled over as well.

We tied up as soon as possible, and the deck trailers were cleared off in record time to allow the vets and cattlemen access to the poor animals. The RSPCA turned up as well, and all the ship's staff helped out as best we could with the distressing situation.

Several months later, I received a summons to appear in the Magistrates' Court charged with cruelty to animals. Under the Livestock Act, I was the responsible person – the buck always stops with the Master, no matter what. So it was off to the Company lawyers – coincidentally the very same company I had dealt with over those two rig accidents. When I entered their foyer, I was greeted like a long-lost family member and ushered into a beautiful office.

'What have you got for us now? What sort of rig has sunk?' asked the senior lawyer, rubbing his hands together in expectation.

'Twenty cows,' I replied.

He looked glum – not much money for the law firm this time around. Eventually common sense prevailed and the Magistrate let me go, but that's another story.

SCENIC FLIGHT
OVER BURNIE

I was Master of a ship stuck in Burnie, Tasmania, for the weekend, and the Chief Mate had mentioned that he was thinking about learning to fly on his next leave. Having had my flying licence for many years, I suggested that I hire a plane and we go for a spin – give him a bit of hands-on experience.

I'd hired a plane and flown from Wynyard several times before, so it was easy to organise. We headed off in a borrowed car to collect our plane, a pretty well-used, though sound and airworthy, Cessna 172.

We jumped in, got belted up and took off into a beautiful clear sky as the coastline of Northern Tasmania stretched out ahead of us. Once we were stable, I suggested to the Mate that he reach under his seat, lift the bar and slide himself forward to get his feet on the rudder pedals.

Unfortunately, to help pull himself forward, he grabbed hold of the control yoke. He pulled it back (I'd never seen one come out so far!) and the little Cessna turned vertical, straight for the stars. I'd never seen that either!

Several things happened in a very short space of time: I screamed, 'Let the fucking thing go!' The plane stopped, dropped a wing and tumbled. The Mate let go at last, but then his seat slid back and off the rails and he ended up on his arse in the back, feet flapping and a terrified look on his face.

I managed to bunt the nose over, get some air over the wings and control surfaces, and started flying again, but it was a scary moment. Concentrating on getting the plane stable again, I almost forgot about the First Mate until I noticed his shoes flapping beside me. There was no way we could get the seat, and him, back upright again, so he had to stay like an upturned beetle for the 20-minute flight back. He changed his mind about learning to fly.

AN OLD DIVER'S TALES

We had a rare quiet Sunday alongside in Burnie, and I went for a walk along the wharf towards the knuckle, the seaward end. Coming towards me was an old bloke with a bit of a limp and a friendly smile, and we struck up a conversation pretty quickly.

He'd come to have a look at my ship, which he'd picked as being something unusual and not common to the port, and I realised very quickly he knew his way around ships and the sea. Turned out he was a professional hard-hat diver and had been the clearance diver for the port authority. He'd learned his trade while in the navy during the Second World War, when hard-hat diving was at its peak. A hard-hat is the big, round copper-and-bronze traditional diving helmet, worn with a baggy dry suit, and heavy weighted boots; none of the fancy frogman rigs for this guy!

This explained the limp; it was the shuffle associated with divers who have been squeezed – meaning they'd had a touch of the bends. I had become aware of this frightening affliction during my time on a salvage ship, and also in the offshore oil industry. 'The bends' is decompression sickness, caused when quick changes in pressure make nitrogen bubbles form in the bloodstream and joints. It's extremely painful and frequently fatal.

We sat and comfortably yarned for a while about anything and everything, and he mentioned that in years past he'd be periodically called upon to do the most horrible of jobs. All of the coastal towns had sewerage systems that ran out into the sea via a large fabricated pipeline or tunnel. On occasions this would block up, then the sewerage system throughout the town would block up and everyone's toilets would overflow – with disastrous results!

The phone would go mad and the diver was urgently requested to suit up and fix it – pronto! So off he'd go in the workboat with his men: one to manage the boat, and the other in charge of the large air-pump that supplied his air via a hose.

Once on the bottom, he'd walk across – walk, not swim – and peer into the large pipe. As expected, the opening would be jam-packed, from top to bottom and also deep inside, with crayfish – hundreds of them. Crayfish and their other crustacean cousins love sewerage – think about that next time you're chowing down on a crayfish, crab or prawn! Over many years of trial and error, he'd discovered that the best implement to manage this problem was a farmer's pitchfork, and the best technique was to hit the blockage hard and never pause!

So away he'd go, shovelling like a madman, and as quickly as he'd shovel the crayfish out, they'd all run back inside the pipe again.

Herding cats?

But the gruelling pace he'd set himself would eventually win the day, and without any warning the high-pressure build-up of shit would explode out, taking him and his crayfish mates out to sea in a mighty rush.

Problem solved.

Except for the fact that his boat crew wouldn't let him back into the boat!

He'd close off the exhaust valve in the helmet and air up his suit to become buoyant, and they would then tow him back to town behind the workboat to wash him down.

Truly, a fearsome day's work, by any standards! Needless to say, crayfish mornay was never on his menu.

THE ANNUAL ROEBUCK BAY
HOTEL RACE

Broome was great before the tourists and grey nomads discovered it. It was raw, wild and exotic. I was lucky enough to work out of there for a few years as Master of an AHSV: one of the best jobs I've ever had.

It was a beautiful, powerful ship (the most powerful in Australia at the time), and a great crew – deck seamen, Mates and engineers. This was a very efficient, capable and happy ship, and the clients loved us.

We worked eight weeks on and eight weeks off – two complete crews alternating – and I got on well with the other Master. He'd picked the ship up new from the Carrington shipyards in Newcastle and set everything in place to ensure its working life got off to a good start. Because it was the biggest and most powerful ship in the country at that time, the Master had his crew make up some enormous stencils that said *VENI VIDI VICE*: 'I came, I saw, I conquered'. Apparently Julius Caesar first muttered this in the Senate when describing a recent battle – it could also be found on the Marlboro cigarette packets.

By the time that crew's eight weeks were up and I took over, *VENI VIDI VICE* was stencilled in huge letters above the windows across the bridge front. I thought it looked pretty impressive, but my crew had different ideas. As soon as we joined the ship, my crew got a paint roller and covered the three words up. They then reapplied the stencils in a different sequence. *VIDI VICE VENI*: 'I saw, I conquered, I came'. That set the pace for the next eight weeks. When the leave crew returned, their first task was to reinstate the original wording.

Like all offshore oil ships, this one was always dry at sea. But at port it was an entirely different story, and we developed a reputation as a party ship. It was quite common to have navy patrol boats, fishing boats and cruising yachts all racked up alongside us. Broome, situated in Roebuck Bay, has an extreme tidal range of 10 metres, so as we went up and down with the tide, the other boats would rise and fall with us.

Once a year, the Roebuck Bay Hotel would hold a race. The pub was a classic – big wide verandahs, batwing doors, and an enormous public bar always full of offshore crews, oil rig crews, long-haul truckies, pearl divers, fishermen, navy sailors, yachties, local Indigenous people and anyone else interested in having a blast.

This is how the race worked: a representative from each of the boats in town would front up to the bar where big pints of beer were waiting, as well as three additional schooner glasses per contestant. One was full of baked beans, another held six raw eggs and the third was full of red jelly crystals. You had to scull your beer, followed by one of the other schooners, run out of the bar, around the verandah, and back in for another pint and another commodity.

It took three runs around the verandah to glug down the eggs, beans and crystals, not to mention the litres of beer. Not for the faint-hearted, I can assure you. And there was some fierce competition: some of the yachties and fishermen hadn't had a decent meal for weeks so the 'food' looked good to them, and you should never, ever get between anyone in the navy and a free beer.

I was chosen to represent my ship and lined up at the bar. The gun went bang and I did my best with the bucket of beer. I was only halfway through when I noticed others were already gagging down the eggs and running out the door. I pushed myself harder and joined the melee – pushing, shoving, punching and tripping were all acceptable. I pushed some yachtie over the edge of the verandah and onto the road, and smashed through the batwing doors.

On this second round I got the beer down, but someone had already glugged down my baked beans. The crowd was roaring, so I had no choice but to up-end the half-litre of red jelly crystals. Everything was going well until the red jelly crystals, six raw eggs, and 3 litres of beer combined with cataclysmic results. This vomit wasn't so much 'projectile' as 'exploding' all over the bar and what was left of the beans.

I felt near death when a huge trawlerman burst through the door only to find his final glasses awash with my spew. Being a gentle, caring person, he grabbed me by the neck and flung me across the bar, threatening to do terrible things to what was left of me. 'You fucking bastard!' he roared. 'I've been practising all year for this.'

I slithered out of striking distance as sporadic fights broke out. The race was cancelled. The spectators were very pissed off, and the crews of the other boats were ready to kill. The inevitable, massive, free-for-all ensued while I was left alone, in disgrace, guts still churning as I sat in a big red puddle of my own making.

Everyone went home happy. What a great day out!

A HERCULEAN EFFORT

We were alongside in Broome, sitting outside with our feet on the rail, enjoying a well-earned beer or two, when we noticed a station wagon pull up containing four guys, all checking us out.

Broome is a friendly place, and we were friendly people, so we invited them aboard to take a look at the ship. It turned out they were the flight crew of an Airforce C130 Hercules, and they were flying a big group of army officers around the coast to inspect various installations. As the army officers preferred their own company, the four flight crew members were left to their own devices. So they hired a car and found us.

They had a huge purpose-built esky full of beer in the station wagon, and we ended up having a big night with a lot of laughs. I was a keen pilot myself and loved hearing their stories. When it was time to go, they started picking up all the empty cans and throwing them in their esky.

'Don't worry about that,' I said. 'We'll fix that up in the morning.'

But, no. They had a purpose for the cans, and it would help them get some revenge on the uppity army officers. The plan was that every 15 minutes or so on the way from Broome to Darwin, they would open the cockpit door and chuck three of four empty cans out. By the time they got to Darwin, the terrified officers would be up to their knees in empties.

The next morning, we were standing out on deck with a cup of coffee when we heard the Herc's engines spooling up, then a roar as the four turboprops went to full thrust and the monster took off. We couldn't see anything and presumed they were on their way to Darwin.

But then, over the sand dunes, the Herc came straight at us at full noise, missing the top of our mast by what felt like inches – what a rush! I hope the army officers thought so, too.

THE BANK
TELLER'S PANTS

It had been a long day preparing to depart for Singapore towing a semi-submersible drill rig from Australia. There was a mountain of paperwork for customs and immigration, and endless detail about food stores, fresh water, laundry, fuel, lube oil, spare parts, charts etc.

By the day's end, most of the crew had quietly slipped over to the pub for a final beer before the long, dry voyage to Singapore. My work finally completed, I managed to dash across for a quick drink myself. As I approached, I heard the pub was in full cry, in typical North West Australian fashion. I pushed through the batwing doors to find the place heaving with ships' crews and miners, all jostling and slopping pots of beer and roaring encouragement to an impromptu billiard tabletop dancer who I recognised as a teller from the bank. Just then, someone up-ended a jug of beer over the dancer's head, which only encouraged her more. As the crowd roared, she slid off a sexy pair of black panties, twirled them around her head and threw them into the crowd. The roof nearly lifted off!

The beer-soaked panties flew through the air and there was a huge skirmish of grabbing hands. The successful catcher was a huge tall bloke – one of my ABs! He fought off a few combatants by clubbing them with his oversized fists and, with great show, crammed the panties into his mouth and swallowed them down with a huge swill of beer. The crowd went cheering, screaming, beer-slopping crazy.

WTF! I was horrified! Not because of the teller and the ease with which she dropped her pants, but at the thought of a long, slow ocean tow, well outside of helicopter range, and an AB with a blockage in his guts. As the only trained person onboard it would fall upon me to slice him open when he jammed up.

My AB was revelling in his new-found hero status and was having trouble chugging down the free beers being thrust upon him. I pushed my way through the heaving, sweaty crowd and eventually managed to scream in his ear.

'Yep, Captain,' he yelled back. 'I swallowed 'em down, no problem!'

Fucking great, I thought. I finished my beer, which now tasted like shit, and fought my way to the door then back to the ship. I got on to a doctor at the Base Hospital and told him that I was the Master of a ship and needed some advice.

'One of my ABs just swallowed a sheila's panties in the pub, and we are off on a long ocean voyage,' I told him.

There was a long silence, followed by, 'What the fuck?'

Not very professional, I thought. I told him that I'd recognised the woman, that she was a bank teller. He seemed to be familiar with her.

'Were they cotton or nylon?' he said.

'How the fuck would I know!' I replied.

'It makes a big difference,' he said, 'because if they're cotton they might break down. Nylon won't, and the elastic will be a problem, too, because it could cause a serious obstruction and require surgery. You could ring her husband and ask him; I know his number,' said the doctor.

That's a great idea, I thought. I'd bet he'd just love to know that his wife is pissed in a waterfront bar throwing her panties to the crowd! WTF.

Next call was to my boss, the marine manager.

'Sounds like you've got a problem, 'cos there's no way we can get a replacement up there, and you can't sail short-handed – hope you're handy with a scalpel!' *Click.*

Back to the hospital again, and this time the doctor was a little more helpful. He told me there was a reasonable chance the AB may survive if he could pass the panties through his system.

'He's a dirty great big fucking Yugoslav,' I said.

'They're a pretty tough breed,' said the doctor. 'He should be able to shit 'em out in a day or so – hopefully.'

Lot of science, experience and logic went into that assessment, I thought. So, the next morning it was business as normal, as we pulled away from the wharf and headed out to the anchorage to get the rig underway. In the messroom, I made a point of finding my man.

'Anything yet, mate?'

'No, nothing yet, Captain,' he said. 'I'll try again and push a bit harder.'

After two days and no reports of pain or interesting finds in the toilet bowl, I could start to relax a little and put *The Ship Captain's Medical Guide* back in the bookshelf. Thank God for cotton panties.

FAMILY LIFE

A life at sea can mean months away from home, which can be tough for families, but it also gives you months of leave, and my wife Sandy and I always took full advantage of that time.

We bought a block of land, and I planned and drew up a house myself and built it together with my brother-in-law (a carpenter). We're still in it now. Two beautiful daughters came along, and we made a very conscious decision to live our life to the fullest while the children were still young. We didn't want to wait till we were 50 years old with 25-year-old children before we travelled the world together.

So instead of buying carpet for the house, we lived in Fiji and Hong Kong for a while; instead of buying a new car, we went camping and boating and did anything else that took our fancy. We took the girls out of school whenever it suited us and chased dreams. We had a trailerable yacht and I bought my first aeroplane, a small single-engine Piper Warrior. The kids would be bundled in the back of the plane, each with a plastic bag hooked over their ears to spew in. Sandy would hold the map – which was more of a formality, as we never really planned where to go: we just went.

The work/leave cycle worked well for all of us and allowed me to spend a lot of quality time with my children. There were always challenges, and coming home usually took a short period of adjustment – though I can safely say I never had an adjustment period quite as awkward as my friend Pete once did.

After a gruelling four-week swing in The Patch, Pete was glad to be home and on steady ground. His wife was off for her weekly tennis catch-up with her girlfriends and Pete had plans to meet up with some shipmates for a boozy lunch. Life was good!

The lunch turned into a monstrous piss-up, and on returning home by cab, Pete thought it might be wise to rack out on the bed for a while before his wife got home. So he kicked off his gear and passed out on the matrimonial bed.

Waking with a start, Pete felt violently ill. He dived for the door and raced to the bathroom but realised he wouldn't make it – the kitchen sink would have to do. He launched into a mighty spew with convulsions that racked his whole body and ended with a long, drawn-out fart. Only then did he get the horrifying sense that there were other people in the room.

Dressed only in a T-shirt and one sock, everything limply hanging out, he slowly turned around and wiped the spew from his chin. There was his wife and four of her tennis friends at the table having coffee.

'Meet my husband, Pete.'

MAJOR THE CLYDESDALE

Bluewater seafarers and farmers are totally different beings, anatomically. A sailor cannot sit on a horse; they are designed in a different way and have neither the ability nor desire to change. Many have tried, and failed.

My wife and two young daughters loved horseriding and wanted to get me involved, but they weren't going to convince me. I like horses, and any other animals for that matter – just don't ask me to ever get on the fucking thing! Then I came across an offshore oil man who had a small business hiring out horse-drawn Gypsy-style caravans in an area of Victoria not too far from our home. Seemed like a good compromise: four wheels, and a horse.

So a booking was made for a four-day trip with my family; their ponies were bundled into the horse float and away we all went to collect the caravan. My wife and myself decided to make it an alcohol-free holiday.

When we arrived at our destination and ran the ponies off the float, we were excited to see our new home for the long (very long!) weekend: a bright yellow-and-green

Gypsy wagon with modern car wheels and tyres instead of traditional spoked coach wheels – and nicely fitted out inside like a small caravan.

Standing aside was a fucking big horse: a Clydesdale named Major. We made eye contact, and it was hatred at first sight.

The owner gave us a briefing, and in a very short time Major was rigged up and ready to go, with the kids on their ponies streaming off the port and starboard quarters of the caravan. A map was provided and a campsite would be prepared for our arrival at the riverbank.

It started off fine. The Gypsy caravan was well built, with its modern car wheels, axles and hubs together with a basic hydraulic braking system taken from a wrecked car. The small brake pedal on the floor worked fine, and I was able to relieve the weight of the coach on Major by squeezing on a bit of drag. We jogged along at a sedate pace and the kids dashed around on their ponies, now and then tying them up to the wagon and running alongside to jump in. It would have been perfect with a can of beer or a glass of wine …

Eventually we arrived at a crossroad where two dusty gravel roads met somewhere in the middle of the state forest. I unrolled the chart to take a look, but Major was already on the move to take the left road. My chart clearly showed that straight ahead was the course line we needed, and no goddamn fucking horse was going to tell me, a professional and experienced navigator, which way to go!

Major kept the pressure up to turn left, but I soon mastered the beast and we headed off straight ahead, as the map clearly showed. After a few long and dusty hours we crested a hill and looked straight down a very steep descent that crossed a small culvert, and then went straight up the other side. Seemed a bit of a challenge, but not impossible.

It took quite a bit of encouragement to get Major to move, but we entered the steep slope and commenced the descent with the kids tagging along on their ponies.

Suddenly, the brakes totally failed. The pedal went to the floor and no amount of pumping would give any pressure at all. The full weight of the heavy wagon heading downhill now fetched up on the breaching strap fitted around Major's arse, and going by his quivering muscles – and a few farts – he wasn't handling this shock load too well.

Wife and kids then abandoned ship to the roadway; probably a wise move!

As Major braced himself against the load, it crossed my mind that all would be okay if Major could slowly get us to the bottom, hopefully without losing the plot and breaking into a gallop.

Just as I was mulling over this, Major took off at a furious pace! He tore off down the steep hill with 2 tonnes of yellow-and-green Gypsy van flailing around behind, and me braced across the seat in sheer terror. Major, followed by the van, hit the culvert at breakneck speed, and then shot up the equally steep opposite side. The inertia kept us going for a while, but soon Major was fucked and stopped dead on the steep incline with his legs braced and muscles twitching.

It quickly became obvious that he couldn't hold us on the steep incline anymore, and his massive legs and feet started to scrabble as the wagon now started to roll slowly backward downhill.

WTF.

I bailed out and found a big rock to wedge under the wheel, and Major let the load ease back and gave me a dirty look. A few more rocks behind all four wheels and the job was secure, but Major looked pretty fucked by the experience.

He then let go a massive shit; and I was pretty close to doing the same!

What to do now?

After we let Major catch his breath, I eased him into dead slow ahead and he took the weight. With a mighty fart, Major leaned into the job and slowly started the long climb uphill, the ponies trailing astern, while we ran alongside with rocks ready to chock the wheels, just in case.

It was a great relief to make it to the top, and we all paused to take a deep breath – I needed a beer, a great big one, and so did Major by the look of him.

Off we went again, and things settled down, with my wife in the back reading a magazine and kids dashing around on their ponies. The homemade map still didn't make much sense to me, but Major seemed to be steaming along okay now; all's well.

I'd always been a bit of a petrol-head and had a pretty good ear for a racing engine at full noise. Which was exactly what I started to hear – how strange. The next instant, my vision (and Major's) was filled with a rally car at full speed drifting around the corner and coming straight at us!

I could clearly see the look of horror on both the driver and navigator's helmeted faces as they were faced with a windscreen full of Clydesdale and Gypsy cart. With a thunderous fishtailing of gravel, the rally car swept down our side and shot round the bend!

I pulled over to the side of the road as more rally cars sped past, but finally a car load of very angry officials turned up. They'd been called up on the UHF radio by a very distressed rally driver who had been assured that this closed section of road had been 'swept' and was clear to race.

Big surprise for all of us!

Somehow we had blundered onto the closed road; probably made a wrong turn somewhere ...

We were then sent off on a side road that eventually led straight onto a four-lane highway. I had a bit of trouble carrying out a U-turn across all four lanes with Major's wide turning circle: terrifying for me, and even more so for the high-speed traffic going in both directions! Major didn't give a fuck.

After a very long day's travel, we somehow arrived at the designated campsite by the river, greeted by a very hostile campsite owner who had been driving all over the forest looking for us – but he went pretty quiet when I told him of our day's experiences!

Major and the ponies were made fast to a long line and fed, and we lit up our campfire and settled down for the evening.

My wife and I both now desperately needed alcohol.

We shut the van up for the night and the girls were snuggled into bed. I folded out my bed on the covered deck, climbed aboard and promptly fell on my arse as the whole apparatus collapsed. After a fitful few hours curled up on the hard floor like a dog, I awoke to familiar and lovely sounds – drunks shouting and screaming and car engines roaring. The local yobbo population had arrived after the pub shut and were settling into a night of festivities by the riverbank. As the hours rolled by and the noise got louder, it slowly dawned on me that we were extremely vulnerable. I explained to my increasingly terrified wife that our bright yellow-and-green Gypsy wagon parked on a gently sloping riverbank might become a tempting target for some fun and games.

I crouched by the door for the remainder of the night armed with a serrated breadknife from the kitchen drawer, ready to pounce – but nothing happened. I found out later that we were, in fact, very safe, as the local yobbos had a healthy respect for the wagon owner and his extremely violent temper.

I crawled out in the morning feeling like a busted arse, with the worst kind of hangover you can get: a totally alcohol-free hangover. After breakfast, Major was rigged up and off we set for the long drag home. No more twisting roads through the forest, just the most direct route home down dead-straight roads. With a long straight road, I thought it would be easy enough to tie Major's reins to a cleat and lay back for the ride.

No way.

Major was now set on revenge, and every time I released my hold on the reins he'd stop dead and wouldn't move until he was sure I held them again. I tried everything I could think of but to no avail; Major wanted me to suffer, and suffer I did.

It was a very long drag home, and it was a great relief to arrive and drop anchor.

The caravan's owner was pleased to see us, too, I think. He thoughtfully offered us a 10 per cent discount for next time we booked.

Not in this fucking lifetime, mate!

The ponies were run into the float in record time and away we went, straight to the nearest pub.

SCISSORS, STAT!

When you're Master on a ship and a medical emergency arises, *The Ship Captain's Medical Guide* is all you have. It's a huge book with lots of big pictures, mainly of syphilitic cocks, damaged eyeballs, and – strangely enough, in those days at least – a section on childbirth. But 'The Book' still sometimes let me down.

It was a nice sunny day somewhere in the Southern Ocean, and we were towing a semi-submersible oil rig, not a care in the world. Suddenly (it's always suddenly), the bridge door burst open and there was the chief engineer, clutching a bloodstained rag to his guts. When he took the rag away, I saw a long corkscrew of red meat dangling out of a perforation in his belly. He told me he had been using a cordless drill on the engine-room workbench when he pushed down hard and the drill bit slipped, drilling a bit of meat out of his stomach. Hmmmm. Time to get out The Book. Unfortunately, the index had nothing to say about dangling guts.

The wiggly worm of red meat was about 50 millimetres long, and I tried to poke it back in with the chart pencil, but it kept popping out again. The piece didn't look too vital, so I snipped it off with scissors, gave it back to the chief as a souvenir and stuck a bandaid over the wound. The chief engineer went away happy and everything returned to normal.

NORMAL PEOPLE

We'd had a hard few weeks working a 'gorilla' hostile environment semi-submersible drilling rig in the Great Australian Bight, with big heavy gear, 12 monstrous anchors and very, very rough weather. But my ship was well suited to the task: German-built, heavy, powerful, it was an A1+ icebreaker with all the gear. I loved it!

It was great to finally be released by the drilling superintendent and to head back to Port Lincoln for some maintenance, stores and back cargo. The body is saying, 'turn in, and have a big sleep', but the brain is saying, 'let's have a drink!' Brain wins.

On the way back after one too many pubs, I could see the ship's lights in the distance and was reassured to know it hadn't caught fire or sunk in my absence. I ducked down a laneway for a quick leak when suddenly the place lit up with the glare of a police patrol's spotlight.

'What are you doing?' boomed the voice.

In the position I was in, holding what I was, I would have thought it was obvious. But they kept hammering me with questions before sternly sending me on my way, warning, 'Don't pull that thing out again in Port Lincoln.' Friendly town!

I made it back to ship, mission accomplished. When I woke the next morning, I made a cup of strong coffee and stepped out onto the small deck space outside the Master's cabin to take in the fresh morning air. Leaning on the handrail, I looked down to the gangway and noticed a gang of schoolkids on their bikes. They'd obviously come down to look at the big, tough-looking ship, but were distracted by something else. Sprawled on the gangway was one of my IRs, unconscious, with spew all down the front of his company overalls (great advertisement for P&O Energy Services), topped off with six squawking seagulls all feeding on the spew.

What a story to take to school!

That day dragged like you wouldn't believe, and I was relieved to hit the sack early. I was dozing off when I heard, 'Captain, please come quickly, someone's been hurt!' I pulled on some clothes and made my way down a couple of decks to the messroom. What a sight!

There were blood splatters and droplets everywhere, and an impressive Hollywood-inspired bloody handprint smeared down the bulkhead. The six IRs were all sitting very quietly and calmly, angelic expressions on their faces.

'What the fuck is going on?' I asked.

'Nothing, Captain, all under control – nothing to worry about. Just a misunderstanding. We'll have it cleaned up pronto.'

I crawled off back to my cabin and quickly went back to sleep.

'Captain! The coppers are in the messroom and want to speak to you!' WTF!

It seemed that the boys had another, this time more *meaningful* misunderstanding and used the galley carving knives to prove their points.

'Who are you?' asked the copper.

I'm the Master, I replied.

'The what?'

'The captain,' I explained.

'Hang on, aren't you the bloke we caught pissing between the shops last night? What sort of crazy fucking ship is this?' said the copper to his mate. 'Are there any normal people onboard?'

Probably not, but it was pretty much just a normal day on an offshore anchor-handler, really.

SHEEP CARRIER

The live export of sheep and cattle doesn't sit well with anyone, including seafarers. But it's big business and there are lots of ships worldwide engaged in the trade, which means lots of problems and incidents, including the biggest of them all: fire.

This big sheep carrier had just left Australia with 30,000 sheep onboard when a fire broke out in a feed hopper and, in a very short time, engulfed the vessel from stem to stern with disastrous results. The penned-up sheep didn't stand a chance. The port authorities wanted it gone ASAP, but since there was no port big enough to deal with this problem in Australia, we were called upon to hook it up and tow the ship to Singapore.

The chief engineer and I went onboard to size the job up, together with a few surveyors and assorted stiffs. The first thing that hit us was the smell of the biggest roast lamb dinner ever made – but this was to change very quickly.

The ship's freeing ports – gaps in the shipside bulwarks to allow water to run off – were festooned with huge stalactites of congealed fat running down the ship's side, and the pens were a nightmare of burned carcasses. A quick look around determined it would be straightforward to connect our 90-millimetre tow wire to the ship's anchor chains, after hanging off the anchors. Things moved rapidly because the port and city wanted this scene of horror gone.

Compared to cumbersome and ungainly oil rigs, ships are simple to tow, and we were looking forward to an easy run, especially with the wind and weather coming from astern. But not long into the voyage it soon became obvious that we had a problem: with 30 thousand sheep carcasses putrefying in the hot sun, the ship took on an almighty stink. And there were clouds of shiny black, fat and greasy flies. The prevailing wind from astern ensured that our ship was perpetually sitting in a bubble of flies and stink. It was horrible. The stench permeated every space, despite the sealed doors and full air-conditioning. Only the most hardened of us could go on deck without gagging. Did I mention the flies?

The only thing I could do was to 'tack' like a yacht in large alternating zigzags to give us some breathing space. This, of course, added days and thousands of dollars in fuel to the voyage. Instead of being an easy run, it had become a slow and incredibly smelly ordeal.

As we got closer to Singapore, it was no longer possible to 'tack' because of coastlines, islands, reefs and increasing ship traffic. Ships approaching from astern to overtake us took serious avoiding actions once they entered the bubble of stench. Finally, we made it to the approach channels of

Singapore. No matter how many times you do it, it's always a hectic day or so dodging the huge numbers of ships passing back and forth in Singapore Strait. It's a lot better now, with tighter traffic controls and vessel reporting systems, but back then it was every man for himself.

The Port of Singapore gave us a clearance for the Western Anchorage and it was a great relief to see a launch full of shore workers clamber aboard, secure her to a swing mooring and slip our tow gear. Free at last, a run ashore for an ice-cold Tiger beer never looked so good.

But the VHF and Satcom suddenly went mad with calls from Singapore Port, our agents, and our owner. It turned out that we had left the sheep carrier upwind of the CBD, and within an hour the city was enveloped in an unbelievable stench and clouds of flies! 'Please come back and move it,' was the cry.

'Not possible. Not possible at all,' I replied. Our contract was completed. If they wanted us back then a new contract would have to be drawn up and executed by our management, not by me. I believe they sorted it out with the use of harbour tugs and took it a very long way away, around the corner somewhere. The things you do for money!

DOD

Sometimes you cross paths with special people who make a big impact on your life and, perhaps, even change your destiny. DOD was one of these people for me. A very professional seafarer, with a good pedigree, he was my boss in the best company I have ever worked for.

In the 1970s, the oil industry was still relatively young in Australia, and business was booming. The industry was hungry for modern, powerful and efficient anchor-handling supply vessels (AHSV), and the shipping companies were hungry for human resources across the board.

The Australian Shipping and Maritime community had never seen anything like this. Conventional shipping was well established: cargo and container ships, ro-ros, tankers and bulkies were operating everywhere at a high level, but the surge in the offshore oil industry caught everyone by surprise. The type of work was different, difficult and dangerous, and the ships were quite odd and strangely configured. They had to be overpowered for their size and extremely manoeuvrable because of the type of close-in work required. The controls from the front of the bridge had to be duplicated at the back of the bridge because 90 per cent of the 'driving' was done backwards.

This strange setup attracted strange people; you either loved the job or loathed it, and many people came for one trip and were never seen again. The industry grew at a phenomenal rate, but finding the right crew became a problem. Although dangerous, the work came with film-star pay and conditions, better leave, and never a dull moment. For example, the work leave cycles on conventional ships at this stage were one for one (one day's leave accrued for one day's work) but on the 'anchor clankers' it was 1.1573 days leave for every day worked and effectively seven months' leave for five months' work per annum. Comparatively the pay was sensational and the conditions – allowances, travel, clothing, study leave etc. etc. were the best in the industry. Plus, promotion was on merit and not on seniority, which was a big incentive considering we all came from a background where you'd have to wait for someone above you to drop dead to gain advancement.

Overarching all of these wonderful things was the fact that the Company was a pleasure to work for, and really cared for its sea staff. The management at all levels and the office staff from top to bottom always made you feel welcome whenever you attended the office. If ever a sea staff wife had a new baby, the first and biggest bunch of flowers was from 'the office'. When my house was in the path of bushfires and

I was away at sea, the Company driver was sent out to help with instructions to 'do whatever was needed'. It was easy to be loyal to a company such as this, and there was a wonderful atmosphere of camaraderie in those early days. All of these things are driven from the top, and my first point of contact was DOD.

I was at this stage a senior Master and in a good place, but an offer came along to join a brand new company driving one of the latest and most powerful ships, managed and operated by close friends. I agonised over it for weeks, but the temptation to drive a state-of-the-art ship proved irresistible.

I set off for the long drive to Melbourne from Nar Nar Goon, found somewhere to park and legged it up Collins Street to the fourth-floor office. DOD was at his desk in the lee of a mountain of files and paperwork, but he welcomed me when he saw me milling about. I stuttered my way through a poor pre-rehearsed excuse as to why I wanted to leave, and DOD just nodded. I found the whole thing very upsetting, especially after the Company, and DOD in particular, had looked after me so well and given me every opportunity for advancement.

DOD was very brief and said that although he was sad to see me go, he would never get in the way of anyone's advancement. I signed off a few bits of paper and scuttled out the door, hugely relieved to have got this out of the way, and headed home. After a very long and thoughtful drive back to the bush, I walked in the door just as the phone started ringing. It was my new boss calling from the Korean shipyard where the new ships were nearing completion.

'Can't talk for long, very busy,' he said, 'but whatever you do don't resign from your job as the new ships have just been sold and I don't have any work for you.' *Click.*

WTF!

I shuffled back into the car, drove back to the city, found a parking spot and dragged myself up Collins Street for the second time that day. DOD peered over his reading glasses and raised an eyebrow.

'What are you doing here?' he said.

'Well, I walked around town for a bit and came to realise that I'd perhaps been a bit hasty, and that I really don't want to leave this great company. I want to stay.'

'It doesn't work that way in the real world ...' said DOD.

I was speechless, frozen in the moment.

'But seeing as I been very busy today and haven't had any time to process your resignation, I will make an exception. You can have your job back and we'll forget it ever happened.'

I backed out of his office, stern-first – a sort of humble, grovelling, crab walk to the door.

'By the way,' he said. 'I knew first thing this morning that those ships had been sold and you didn't have a job to go to. Better be a bit more careful next time, eh?'

That was close!

THE SCANDAHOOLIGANS

I was sent over to Sweden to pick up a ship and deliver it to Singapore. A Swedish Master would come along and help manage the Swedish officers and crew, and my friend Alan came from Australia with me as chief engineer. Alan is a naturally funny guy and has a stutter that makes me laugh whenever he opens his mouth. I'd need that distraction on this voyage.

The ship was called *Gute* (pronounced '*Goo-tah*') after the residents of the island of Gotland, from which bloodthirsty warrior pirates the Goths hailed. *Gute* was a nice ship, a very modern and well-built class-1 icebreaker, and very well looked after. The ship was something of an institution in the town of Visby, where all the crew lived. They'd had an easy job for the past ten years or so: a run of a couple of hours across to Oskarsharm on the coast of Sweden and back again. *Gute* was the sole means of transport to the island and carried about 30 semitrailers and trucks on deck, and containers down below. She was built as an icebreaker because for several months of the year the area iced up to about 2 metres.

The town of Visby itself was fantastic, a historical place to wander around, full of stone buildings and cobbled lanes. Every second door was a bar with loud music and loud people – the whole place was, and still is, a madhouse – just like home to 'jolly jack the sailor'.

After ten years of going back and forth, the crew were very excited to be heading off to Singapore via the Mediterranean Sea and the Suez Canal. We sailed from Visby, farewelled by the whole town and a brass band, down the Baltic and across to Felixstowe in the UK for some equipment. Before setting off again from Felixstowe we loaded some equipment and, more importantly, the Porsche and BMW motorbikes I had bought in England, and off we went again, bound for Singapore.

Down and through the English Channel, past Land's End and straight into a North Atlantic gale – one of the worst in a decade. The *Gute* rolled and pitched and heaved and shuddered, and after a few days of this I was feeling a bit queasy: very delicate indeed.

One morning, I opened my cabin door and was smacked in the face by the most horrific fucking smell I'd ever encountered (and I've smelled some). The whole ship was saturated in this stomach-churning pong, and when Alan stuck his head out, I could see that he was a distinctive shade of green. We crawled down the heaving, rolling flights of stairs and passageway to the messroom, where the Swedes sat around a plate of seriously rotten canned fish, scooping up the sloppy, putrefying mess with bits of bread. This, apparently, was surströmming (sour herring), a traditional Swedish delicacy that is only ready to eat when the ends of the can blow out by the pressure from the rotting mess inside. WTF! Between this and the heavy weather, I did not feel at all well. We found four more cans of this stuff in the pantry and chucked them over the side.

We clawed our way down the coast of France, and it took three days to get past Spain – we passed the same lighthouse three times in one day. But the storms passed once we got around Gibraltar, and it was an easy run up the Mediterranean. The sun came out, and so did the Swedes.

It must be remembered that the Swedes had just come from a northern winter, and that they're mostly fair-skinned people. Swept up in the excitement of being out of the Baltic, they all appeared on deck in this strange assortment of swimming costumes and started tanning. And drinking. It seemed that Scandinavians didn't drink to be convivial, but to get rip-roaring, piss-your-pants drunk as soon as possible, and then collapse. The weapon of choice was vodka, but drunk warm (in this case heated in the funnel casing on the boat deck) while sitting in the hot Mediterranean sun. You can guess the results.

Within a couple of hours, the deck was sprinkled with a dozen totally hammered Swedes, all lying differently and all burned bright red on one side like sausages on a barbecue.

Some were already blistering, and Alan and I dragged the bodies into the shade where they stayed until sunset. This 'drinking hot, straight vodka in the 40-degree heat' became a daily routine, and they even made a spa using wooden pallets, an old tarpaulin and a compressed air hose. They were having a ball and nothing was going to stop them, not even third-degree burns.

The further you get up the Mediterranean, the shittier it gets, until you reach the penultimate shithole: Port Said and the Suez Canal, which we called the Marlboro Canal (for reasons that will soon become clear). Every time we went up there it was worse. The ships had to pass through the canal in convoys of about ten and follow each other along. Each ship had an Egyptian pilot onboard, and nothing moved until he got his *baksheesh* – his kickback. The usual routine was three cartons of Marlboros and three cases of Scotch. We came prepared but weren't to know that the new chief of customs was a devout Muslim and had banned grog, so the pilot wanted another three cartons of cigarettes instead. He then facilitated a complicated arrangement where I got to buy my own cigarettes from a local dealer at an astronomical price and then give them to him again, plus a transaction fee, and another fee for supply and delivery.

There was a big Soviet container ship in front of us that faced the same problem, which the Russian captain solved pretty quickly by throwing the pilot off the wing of the bridge.

The pilot survived the 30-metre drop okay, but broke his neck when he hit the water. The Russian captain weighed anchor and shot off, never to be seen again.

The Scandahooligan crew, never to let an opportunity pass them by, were into it. They bought every ghastly souvenir: genuine, original papyrus paintings of Cleopatra, 'ancient' coins and artefacts (still with *Made in China* stickers on them).

Finally, the convoy set off, and it was a pleasant couple of days heading up the Suez Canal, watching the world go past. There were camels and donkeys carrying things, mud houses, date palms and local kids all against the desert landscape – all very exotic.

Alan and I kept an eye out for the donkey-fucker, even though we knew he wouldn't be there because there were no passenger ships in our convoy. This guy was a legend, even though I suspect there was more than one operator. Whenever a huge passenger liner came past, a thousand passengers with cameras lining the rail, he would pull up his robe, jump up on a wooden box and (at least by the looks of it) fuck his donkey while enthusiastically waving and blowing kisses to the passengers! He had a team of small boys running up and down collecting the coins the passengers would throw. A priceless moment – once seen, never forgotten.

The voyage was pretty uneventful from Aden, along the bottom of India, and up into Malacca Straits, before a terrifying run down the busiest shipping lane in the world into Singapore Harbour. The small boats bearing all sorts of goods came alongside, and the Swedes bought another truckload of absolutely genuine Gucci threads, Rolex watches, and Viagra tablets.

After we'd tied up at Sembawang Shipyard (strategically located as far as possible from the bright lights of Singapore) I told the agent to make arrangements to get the Skandahooligans off my ship, right now, within 12 hours, or I'd get the police to do it for them. Six weeks of that shit was enough. The Company agreed, provided that Alan and myself stayed onboard for the night until the Australian crew joined. No problem. Peace and quiet.

We now had the *Gute* to ourselves, which was luxurious. Alan suggested he'd whip up a chicken curry, and it brought to mind the last 'chicken curry' we'd had together, from a street vendor at Sembawang Shipyard, where the meat being prepared had distinctive red webbed feet! Seagull.

Just as we popped open the Scotch, the fire alarms sounded. 'F-f-fuck it,' said Alan. 'I bet it's that sensor in the vehicle deck playing up again – I'll n-n-nip down and isolate it from the circuit.'

A few minutes later, the phone rang.

'F-F-fucking f-f-fire!' yelled Alan.

That gets you moving, particularly when there are only two of you onboard a big, complicated ship. Usually, you'd get the shipyard fire team involved, but there was no time. We had to move quickly; very quickly. I raced down the ten flights of stairs, from the very top of the ship to the very bottom, where one end of the vehicle deck was well ablaze. Dirty, oily rags and an overheated electrical shore-supply box were the culprits.

The flickering flames reflected off my uninsured Porsche and BMW bikes. *Just great*, I thought, as I grabbed an extinguisher. It wasn't a really big fire, but it took Alan and me an hour and a half to put it out, and we used nearly every extinguisher available. It was a hard fight and by the end of it we were both badly scared (but not scarred), running on nerves. We were black from head to foot, our reasonably good clothes wrecked, both exhausted with throats parched and eyes burning. I was close to spewing and couldn't stop my leg from shaking.

'Okay,' said Alan, 'how about a nice seagull curry and a hot vodka?'

He didn't stammer, which meant it had scared the shit out of him, too.

LOVE OF THE SEA?

This is a common expression, along with 'He's got the sea in his blood', and a few others. But these phrases are mainly relayed by yachtsmen, coastal fishermen, and other mudhoppers who have never been out of sight of land – and never by true-blue water sailors. Why would you love something that has the potential to smash and kill you?

Of course, I love ships, and the way of life they offer, but not the sea itself. You can only get a true appreciation of the sea, and its vastness, when you're in the middle of it – with no land within a week's steaming in any direction, and 200 fathoms deep. Then you're completely self-sufficient, self-reliant and surviving on your skills, knowledge, experience and professionalism. You're on your own in every respect, and it can be very lonely as a ship's Master. More so in the days before GPS and the internet.

Sure, there are good days. Nice sunny days, calm seas and an endless horizon – at night the starry sky merges seamlessly with the dark ocean. It's a very personal time when you're standing a bridge watch at night, alone on the bridge wing.

But the respect comes when you see the sea in its full fury and ferocity. It has neither feeling nor compassion; it will relentlessly smash everything, and everyone, continuously and without favour.

Love of the sea?

Not me.

'The Mirror of the Sea'

Joseph Conrad

The sea has no generosity.

No display of manly qualities – courage, hardiness, endurance, faithfulness – has ever been known to touch its irresponsible consciousness of power.

The ocean has the conscienceless temper of a savage autocrat spoiled by much adulation.

He cannot tolerate the slightest appearance of defiance and has remained the irreconcilable enemy of ships, and men, ever since ships and men had the unheard-of audacity to go afloat together in the face of his frown.

From that day, he has gone on swallowing up fleets and men without his resentment being glutted by the number of victims – by so many wrecked ships and wrecked lives.

Today, as ever, he is ready to beguile and betray,

to smash and to drown the incorrigible optimism of men who, backed by the fidelity of ships, are trying to wrest from him the fortune of their house, the dominion of their world, or only a dole of food for their hunger.

If not always in the hot mood to smash, he is always stealthily ready for a drowning.

The most amazing wonder of the deep is its unfathomable cruelty.

A RUN ASHORE
TO THE PUB

The big powerful anchor-handler suddenly went deathly quiet as the main engines progressively shut down; only the faint sound of the auxiliary generator could be heard above the whisper of the air-conditioning. After many hard weeks at sea, it was surprising to realise just how much noise the two enormous Nohab Polar diesel main engines actually made. With the bridge equipment and electronics shut down and the ship secure alongside the wharf, I heaved a weary sigh and made my way down the stairs.

'Let's go, come on, Captain Rob, hurry up!' yelled the second engineer, Matt, peeling off his overalls on the run. 'Dave is getting his gear on now, and Eric has got a lend of the nightwatchman's little truck – we'll be ready to roll in ten minutes – pull ya finger out, Captain!'

It was on. Within minutes we were around the watchman's small, beaten-up Toyota tray truck with a couple of old cray pots stacked on the back.

'Chuck them off, jump aboard and let's go,' yelled Dave. With Dave and Eric jammed in the cab, and me and Matt standing up in the back, the Toyota took off with a mighty roar through the gravel car park.

'Give it to her, Dave,' yelled Matt. 'We're on a mission!'

The Toyota skidded out of the car park, the back offside wheel spinning and making smoke, and then took off up the road with an impressive sequence of racing gear changes.

'Hang on tight, for fuck's sake,' I yelled to Matt. 'Dave's in a hurry'.

The truck slid onto the main road, heading into town; the lights of the Continental Hotel were beckoning in the distance. Matt, hanging on with one hand, was crouched like a waterskier. 'Yahoo!' he yelled, and thumped the roof several times in excitement.

When Dave heard the thumps on the roof, he jumped on the brakes. 'Fuck me, Eric, one of 'em must have fallen off! The back wheels locked up, and the Toyota screeched to a stop across the middle of the road.

Unfortunately, Matt did not do the same. He took off over the roof in a classic Superman pose: hands outstretched and feet together. We all watched in awe as Matt flew up the road, straight and level. Then gravity won, and Matt landed and rolled headfirst up the road.

By the time Matt came to a stop, everyone was out of the truck and running to help.

'Fuck,' said Eric. 'Is he okay? There's a fair bit of blood around.'

Matt groaned and rolled into a sitting position, and we quickly gathered him up and plonked him on a nearby park bench.

'Let me have a look,' said Dave, trying not to wince at the sizeable gash on Matt's noggin. 'I've seen worse.'

'You're a fuckwit, Matt,' said Eric. 'Now we're never going to get to the pub.'

'I reckon I can fix Matt's head up with a few stitches,' said Dave. 'How about we race back to the ship, clean him up, and we'll be in the pub in 20 minutes – let's go!' he ordered, stuffing Matt into the cab.

'There are a few bits missing,' said Dave, back in the tiny cabin that was the ship's hospital/dispensary, 'but I reckon I can pull it all together a bit and it should be okay.'

He didn't sound very confident but the pub clock was ticking, so nobody interfered.

'Hey, Dave,' said Matt, 'I noticed that I've got the start of a bald patch – do ya reckon you could pull it up a bit tighter 'round there, mate? To cover it up?'

'No problem, mate,' said Dave. 'I'll give it a go; looks pretty simple, no big deal.'

Dave used eight different suture kits and made a web of threads crisscrossing the very messy area of Matt's injury. He hadn't yet tied any of them off, planning as he was to draw all the bits together at the end.

'Shit, Dave,' I said, 'I have a bald spot coming, too. Can you give me a quote?'

He didn't respond, a picture of total concentration. 'Ready,' he said, 'come here, Eric, and yank on a few of these.'

Progressively they tightened the threads and the wound closed together – well, sort of. Unfortunately, there was an unplanned side effect.

'Fuck me!' said Eric. 'His ears are moving upwards, and so are his fucking eyebrows!'

'Keep going, Eric, don't stop!' yelled Dave.

'He's going to end up looking like Mickey fucking Mouse!' Eric laughed. 'With the ears on top of his head!'

'How's the bald bit look, Dave?' said Matt, his raising eyebrows making it seem all the more plaintive. 'Is it any better?'

'Yeah yeah, good,' said Dave. 'Okay, let's clean him up a bit and get cracking – who needs a beer?'

We bundled back into the truck and off to the pub, slightly more subdued the second time around.

'What the fuck's the matter with him?' said the bouncer, pointing at Matt. 'He can't go in looking like that – he looks a bit fucked ...'

The bouncer took Matt's hat off, and Matt just stood there with blood trickling down his cheeks, a startled deer-caught-in-the-headlights look and ears that had very definitely migrated upwards.

'He looks a bit crazy, too. Is he pissed?' said the bouncer.

'Not yet!' said a chorus.

'No way is he coming in. He looks like he's been in a horror movie.'

'How about if we stick his hat back on?' said Dave.

'No fucking way. You guys are okay, but not the freaky-looking one,' he said.

'Yer on ya own,' said Eric pushing past the bouncer and steaming towards the bar.

Dave and I just looked at each other.

'It's okay, Rob,' said Dave. 'I'll take fucking Matt to the hospital.'

Half an hour later, Dave returned without Matt.

After chugging half a beer, he said, 'The emergency nurse came out and said, "What on earth happened here?" "I dunno," I said, "I just picked him up down the road. He'll explain – I think he's pissed."'

WHEN PUSH COMES TO SHOVE

I was called upon to run a brand new DP2 AHSV from Singapore to West Africa. It was to be a long voyage through Malacca Straits, then across the Indian Ocean passing the Seychelles, between Madagascar and Mauritius, 'round the Cape of Good Hope and back up the West African coast. Then stopping at Walvis Bay (Namibia) then on to Cabinda (Congo) and finally Malongo (Angola).

The Singapore shipyard had fitted all 30 of the large bridge windows with very expensive 25-millimetre Lexan shields so that the rocket-propelled grenades favoured by the pirates would 'bounce' off before exploding. Unfortunately, the big windscreen wipers were now behind the Lexan shields and totally fucking useless against the heavy tropical rain in Malacca Straits. I couldn't see a thing; it was a very long 36 hours with high-density traffic and threats of pirates, so it was a great relief to round the western tip of Indonesia (Banda Aceh) and shape up for the long haul across the Indian Ocean to the Cape of Good Hope.

On deck we had two brand new 30-metre-high speed crew boats as cargo. Big, fancy and expensive, sitting in their purpose-built lifting frames and destined for use transferring rig personnel back and forth in the West African oilfields. Out of the protected waters of Malacca Straits, we punched straight into heavy weather: both wind and waves, but also a heavy swell. Our ship heaved, rolled, yawed and pitched – all at the same time. It was very uncomfortable and set to last 20 miserable days.

The officers were European – the Mates from Slovenia and the engineer officers from Russia – and the crew were Indian, a common configuration nowadays. All seemed to be okay except for the cook, who not only couldn't cook, but was filthy dirty as well.

After a few days, the Indian Bosun came to see me. He was a good hand and I liked him from the start for the way he handled the deck crew, and the reliable way he went about his work in the hectic days before sailing. He was a handsome dude, and extremely polite.

'What's the problem, Bosun?'

'I push,' he said. 'I push and I push. All crew push and push. Cook is very bad and doesn't do his job. Push is very big problem for all crew.'

'What are you talking about?' I said.

Bosun pulled some faces and made a straining motion, with lots of groaning.

'Push, push!' he cried.

I eventually got the picture – and it wasn't good. It seemed that a certain seed was used a lot in their meals, and if this seed was not well cooked in oil, and properly prepared, it resulted in serious constipation.

The Indian crew were very unhappy with this state of affairs. It got progressively worse, and the very angry Russian chief engineer demanded I fix the problem immediately or he'd throw the cook over the side. I pointed out that sacking the cook mid-voyage was a terrible idea – he could do something to the food supplies for starters – and that throwing him over the side was not an option.

I alleviated the problem somewhat by rostering an AB alongside the cook at all times, because there wasn't much the deck crew could do in the very heavy weather anyway.

We banged on south, with a bit of west, closing the coast of South Africa, and the weather was getting even worse because of a deep 990 hPa low south of the cape. I was probably a bit tired and not paying enough attention to detail as I adjusted the voyage plan and course to get us closer to the African coast and hopefully better weather. At about 2am, while I was in my bunk, the ship took a mighty dive, pile-driving down into a hole in the sea, then reared skywards as she climbed back out. Best alarm clock in the world is when you think you're going to die.

I made my way to the bridge, which was a shambles with equipment, books and charts all over the place. All but one of the Lexan window shields had been ripped from their mounting bolts. The bridge officer and crew looked at me wide-eyed. I knew what had happened, and it was my fault. Instead of laying off track lines that got us across the Agulhas current as quickly as possible, we had lingered too long in the area in which the strong south-west winds meet the southbound current head-on. This reaction causes rogue waves up to five storeys high, and, as this particular wave approached, the water underneath the vessel was pulled from under it, leaving a 'hole' that the vessel fell into. We were lucky; our strong, modern, very tough ship got through it okay.

Rounding Cape Agulhas, the southernmost tip of South Africa (not the Cape of Good Hope, which is further up the west coast) is always symbolic, as all the courses from there on are northerly for a change. Also the TV and mobile phones kick in, and it feels like you're back in the world again.

A day or so up the coast, I adjusted our speed for a daylight arrival off Walvis Bay. Twelve hours out, the main engines suddenly shut down – a very confronting silence after 20 days of roaring at full service speed.

A very sheepish-looking chief arrived on the bridge to announce, 'Fuel finished – no more – all gone.' WTF? Fuel figures need careful attention, and although I had quizzed him before departure about fuel onboard, fuel consumption, useable fuel and endurance, it was now apparent he didn't have a fucking clue, but was too Russian-proud to admit it.

'Fuel onboard' is the figure the bean counters like. This is the total amount of fuel on the ship, and at dollars per litre it has a measurable value for use in accounting, such as on-hire, off-hire and other chartering purposes. The only figure navigators (and chief engineers!) need to be 100 per cent sure of is 'useable fuel' – how much fuel can actually be used. This is always a different figure to fuel onboard because not all fuel can be sucked out of a tank. What is left might still have a dollar value, but it won't run an engine.

I couldn't believe a chief engineer could make such a stupid fucking mistake, and that I had stupidly believed every word he said without cross-checking it myself. The buck stopped with me.

We still had fuel, but it couldn't be pumped out by the usual fuel management system, so some fucker would have to open up the various tank manholes and suck out what was left with a small portable Jabsco pump – bucket by bucket, if necessary. It took all day and was a hard, shitty job for them, but eventually I heard both main engines restart, then be run up to full power again. A pleasant sound, you might think? Not to me; I was furious!

With minimal fuel remaining onboard, running two main engines was very stupid; we could easily make the ETA on one engine/one propeller, which halves the fuel consumption – as the goddamn fucking chief engineer should have known himself. I knew I was starting to lose it. Twenty-eight days of heavy weather, violent motion and poor sleep, surrounded by dickheads and day-to-day decisions and dramas had just about done me in. Being Master can be a very lonely job.

The next day arrived warm, sunny and calm. It was a great relief to see the breakwater of Walvis Bay, but I had one more job to do.

'Bosun! Get the cook to the bridge, now!'

Cook appeared on the bridge in his grubby tunic and dirty shoes. 'You're sacked,' I said. 'Get the fuck off my ship as soon as it's alongside.' He didn't have the chance, though, because, as I put the ship alongside, and before any mooring lines or gangway went ashore, out of the corner of my eye I saw a suitcase go flying through the air and land on the wharf, quickly followed by a flying ex-cook.

SOMETHING *OFF* IN THE GALLEY

I was delivering a ship from Singapore to Norfolk Island. It was set to be a long, slow voyage on a scruffy ship with an even scruffier crew and I wasn't looking forward to it. Just before we passed through the Torres Strait, I got a call from the marine manager informing me that my father had killed himself. The manager was very compassionate and seemed a bit confused by my lack of response.

That evening, I went out alone onto the bridge wing and watched the tropical sun slowly set on the emerald-green horizon, followed by twilight, then a universe full of stars. I felt nothing, and I remember having to make a conscious decision to become upset. To somehow shed a tear. My mind was blank. Too much harm had been done, and the only feeling I could muster was one of sadness for lives lost forever.

I found out later that my father and my ex-girlfriend from New Zealand had moved to the UK and made a good life for themselves. She had apparently died suddenly after the discovery of a very aggressive cancer. The following day, he had put a hose from the exhaust into the window of his BMW and drunk a bottle of scotch until the gas did its job. When the police went to his house, they found it had been totally cleared out, scrubbed and polished: just as any good sailor would do when leaving a ship.

Fifty years or so of marine salvage journals, memorabilia, pictures, photographs, awards and artefacts had all gone – most likely he had taken them to the local tip as part of his preparations. I had been written out of his will decades ago and got nothing, as anticipated. That suited me just fine.

We eventually arrived and cleared through Noumea, New Caledonia (as there is no port or harbour on Norfolk Island) and I was glad to have something to do. Our charter was to lay the four 'shore ends' of the sub-sea communications cables terminating in picture perfect Anson Bay, found halfway down the Western coastline of Norfolk Island.

Only the chief engineer and I were Australian; everyone else onboard was Indonesian. The international communications company supplied its own deck crew and management, a team of Poms who lived ashore on Norfolk but came back and forth by launch, staying onboard for the day with lunch provided, and returning ashore each night.

Work had been progressing steadily, and with three weeks left it seemed likely that we'd get the job finished on time. My company would be pleased.

The ship was scruffy, flogged out, and way down the totem pole compared with the current breed of AHSVs. In my usual position at the bridge aft control station, I could look down on the long work deck, three decks below, and keep an eye on what was going on. We were right inside Anson Bay, inshore of the surf line, and you could easily see the bulldozers on the beach hauling our recovery lines ashore. A very pretty sight to see: bright-blue sea reflecting off the shallow sandy bottom, golden beach and the rich, green pines lining the clifftops of Norfolk Island.

I remember thinking it was a very nice day before there was a brief flurry of activity on deck and I noticed the Pommy Bosun running around and waving his arms about. In an instant, the launch was called alongside and all the Poms took off ashore. *What the fuck is going on?*

The bridge door burst open and in charged a red-faced and very angry Pommy manager, babbling about wankers. After he calmed down, I managed to get the gist of what happened, and it wasn't good. It seemed that the Pommy Bosun went into the galley to make a cup of coffee and found the cook preparing some kind of slop for lunch with one hand and masturbating one of the sailors with the other! With a mighty shriek, the Pommy Bosun dropped his cup and ran out on deck to tell his men that lunch was off – really off! And away they went. Job over. WTF.

I had to let my boss in Melbourne know ASAP. There were no satellite phones then, so it was a case of going through

Norfolk Island radio on HF radio; not the clearest form of voice communication at the best of times, especially when you're tucked away in the lee of Anson Bay.

The boss came online with a mighty burst: 'What the fuck is going on there? I've just been told the ship is off-hire and the client has packed up and left!?'

Between the broken radio and his ranting it was hard to get a word in edgeways.

'Don't you fucking call me a wanker,' he roared. 'I'll have your job and you'll be on the first flight out of there.'

'No, no!' I yelled back. 'I wasn't calling you a wanker. I was trying to explain that the fucking cook was wanking an AB in the galley.'

There was a pause as this information sank in.

'What the fuck?' he said. 'What sort of ship are you running there? Sounds like you've lost the plot. Have you been on the piss, or something?!'

Eventually, after a very long and frustrating phone call, the boss got the picture, although it didn't make him any happier. It didn't sound good, no matter how I packaged it. After much tense negotiating, I managed to get the Poms back onboard, but from then on they brought their own sandwiches and thermoses and we *all* steered clear of the galley.

SNAKE EYES

I was part of a run crew that delivered a big cargo liner to the shipbreaking yard in Taiwan. Instead of flying directly home, a bunch of us decided to come back along the scenic route, via Thailand, the Philippines and Bali.

One day, I was sitting under a palm frond umbrella on the beach at Pattaya in Thailand, having a few Singha beers and watching a local blasting up and down on a jet ski. He was obviously one of the dudes from the jet-ski hire business and very experienced. With a great roar and a flourish, he shot it straight up the beach and stepped off onto the dry sand. Impressive!

Next thing I knew, one of the ship's engineers, Steve, was off doing the same thing: ripping up and down the waterway at a pretty impressive clip – especially for someone who, as we found out later, had never been on one before. The Singha beer was obviously working for him!

Then, from quite a long way out at sea, we heard him wind it up and head straight for the beach. This was really going to be something. Steve had it flat knacker and hit the beach with a mighty thump and a shower of sand. The jet ski came to a very sudden stop when it smacked into a stone wall and exploded into a million pieces. But out of the sand storm, at very high speed, came Steve: first over the stone wall and straight through some roadside bushes, then he seemed to cartwheel across two lanes of traffic before smashing into a group of large, elderly German tourists sitting outside a cafe. Furniture was scattered, drinks sent flying, there were lots of shouts and screams and it was absolute chaos.

Steve was lying unconscious underneath a tangle of chairs and tables, and he was stark naked having been stripped of his shorts on the way through the bushes.

We wandered across to see what could be done and were met with a mighty shriek and a babble of German. We tried to push our way in, but there was another shriek and a German lady fainted – we couldn't see Steve so guessed it was some sort of delayed reaction, though it sounded as if she'd just discovered that the figure had been beheaded!

It turned out it was just that Steve was hung like a horse and had two large snake eyes tattooed on the head of his cock, which was a pretty scary sight by any standards!

THE TRADITIONAL
JAPANESE SPA

I wasn't keen on the idea, but there was no way out. I had three days to spare in Tokyo waiting for a ship to be delivered, and was being looked after by some Japanese friends. One of them arranged a special treat for me at the traditional spa where she worked as a manager.

The 16th-century spa was picture perfect and blisteringly expensive, and if someone like me was just coming off the street, it would be practically impossible to get in the door. Upon entering the spa I came across a fork in the road: women to the left, men to the right. Unfortunately for me, children went with the men. Allocated a locker, I began to undress and realised I was the centre of attention for an audience of wide-eyed, wide-mouthed boys and girls staring in disbelief at my hairy chest, hairy arse and everything in between.

The small, square towel barely covered my cluster, much to the delight of the convoy of children. I made a dash for the pool only to be immediately, but politely, turned back –

'Please, you have to wash first before you jump in the pond.' I sat on a small, very uncomfortable wooden stool to wash and rinse myself, giving my audience a chance for a more detailed inspection.

It was a great relief to finally get my large, pink, hairy body and shrivelled-up little cock into the pool to escape further stares and snickering from the little bastards. That much so that I never noticed the near-boiling temperature of the natural spring water – hot, very hot, fucking unbelievably hot!

I then realised that there were several other blokes floating around in the pool: just heads and bright-red tomato faces sticking out of the water. I noticed that each had his little towel neatly folded on top of his head – so I did the same.

After a while, it dawned on me that I was cooking – I mean really, properly, fucking cooking, and I could feel some body systems starting to shut down. Just before I started slipping into unconsciousness, my friend hauled me out and we headed off towards an incredible igloo, constructed from huge blocks of ice and backlit to produce a beautiful cool blue–green glow. The idea was, like the European spa technique, to alternate between the hot spa and the cold igloo.

Upon entering the igloo, we found about six older Japanese blokes with their tits swinging free, sitting around on the ice benches. All gave a brief, polite nod, and didn't seem to pay too much attention to my now bright-scarlet, hairy, fat body.

But!

As I went to bring my arse to anchor on the ice bench, there was a sudden communal (Japanese) outburst from the group. Easy to interpret, it was something like, 'No! Wait! Aargh, too fucking late!'

As my arse hit the icy seat, I instantly understood their warning, but it was very definitely too fucking late, as my ball sack was now firmly welded to the ice bench. When I looked around at my companions' grimacing faces, I realised that their small towels were no longer on their heads, as mine still was – they were more strategically placed.

Not a lot was said, but there was much sucking of teeth and rolling of eyes.

'No problem,' I said. 'I'm from Australia.' There was much nodding and comment at this news that Australian balls were somewhat different to Japanese balls.

I tried to move a bit to see what the damage was. I managed to rock the arse cheeks free, but the sack was stuck hard and fast, without a millimetre of doubt. Any movement greater than 2 centimetres was going to be eye-wateringly painful, and result in permanent disfigurement.

The final humiliation was that each of my six new-found friends collectively, and individually, decided to carry out a close inspection of the problem, and all seemed to have a different solution – much waving of arms and theatrics. I sat as still and stoically as possible, lips clenched and eyes bulging.

Eventually, a rescue team arrived with a large metal kettle full of warm water, and with a lot of whooping and back-slapping the sack was liberated and my new, naked and baggy-balled friends coached me on the correct way to land your balls on a tiny towel, which is trickier than it sounds.

With the excitement over, and everyone congratulating themselves on a job well done, my friend came along and suggested I accompany him back to the pool for another run. I suggested he stick the spa up his arse, got dressed and fed a shitload of coins into the beer vending machine in the foyer. Never, ever again.

CHRISTMAS CRACKER

I picked up a small tug from a shipyard in Miri, near Brunei, to run across to Singapore.

It was common practice to run these basic new builds across to Singapore where they'd be fitted out with all the electronics and fancy systems, so for this three-day voyage we had no autopilot, and the Indonesian sailors had to take turns at the wheel.

As luck would have it, the weather turned to shit and we found ourselves punching into a heavy sea and swell. As the tug was pretty light (minimal fuel, equipment and stores) she was pretty 'lively', by which I mean totally fucking miserable. It was very uncomfortable, noisy and impossible to sleep, and the food was uniformly atrocious.

In my experience Indonesians are mostly fairweather sailors and not much good in heavy weather, as they get seasick pretty quickly. And so do I. Not actually sick, but pretty close to it – a bit 'fragile'.

The wheelhouse was a good size and was fitted with a very nice chair, bolted to the deck towards the after part of the bridge. There was only one, and it was mine. I spent my bridge time firmly wedged in this chair and watched the heaving, pitching, rolling world go by. I had a good view through the bridge windows and could keep an eye on the helmsman struggling with the wheel as the little ship yawed and swayed.

There is a real art to hand-steering a compass course, and these guys didn't have a fucking clue. Instead of chasing the spinning compass, it's best to sight on something ahead, such as a cloud, and steer for that. Then frequently cross-check with the compass heading. If you chase the compass then the ship will be steering a series of S-shapes from side to side, and not a straight course.

Anyway, it was a fuck-up, but hopefully only for a few days. The ship was rolling very heavily at times, mainly because the dickhead helmsman kept letting the bow fall away, but I was fine in my big chair. Suddenly, the helmsman took a mighty lunge for the wheelhouse door, which, unfortunately for him, was closed and dogged down for the heavy weather. He let go a mighty spew, which hit the door and then bounced back all over him.

I knew that if I got a whiff of this I might be joining him!

He slipped over in the mess and lost his thongs, and then rolled around in it when the ship rolled and he was swept from side to side. The rolling was quickly getting worse now that no one was steering the ship, and it was yawing further across the seaway.

So I left the security of my big chair, took a step over the spew-covered corpse, and used the wheel to steady the ship back on course. Just as I stepped over him, he let go another big spew, which unfortunately reacted at the other end with a massive explosion of shit out the leg of his shorts, referred to in the trade as a 'Christmas Cracker'. That was it for me!

When the power ran off, the little ship lost steerage way and the bow fell away, off the wind. We were now lying across the heavy sea and swell, and she started to roll quite dramatically. While safe, it was very uncomfortable with the roll being quite violent at times. I pulled the engine levers back, let the bow fall away downwind and pushed the emergency station's button.

The Bosun, and others came rushing wide-eyed to the wheelhouse. 'What's the problem, Captain!?'

'That's the fucking problem,' I said as the body washed across the deck in a surge of shit and spew. I just about made it out the door as I left them to it, and spent the next several hours outside taking big deep breaths of fresh sea air. That was a near miss.

A SIMPLE
DELIVERY VOYAGE

My life at sea had taken many shapes. I'd been Master of every type of ship in all parts of the world; survived many years in the offshore oil and gas industry; worked as marine manager for the two biggest OSV companies in Australia, a marine pilot, harbour Master, lecturer, marine consultant, and a few other things along the way. Then for a while I was out of work and unemployed, and actually very happy!

But then along came an opportunity to deliver a series of small tugs to be engaged as chase boats for seismic ships, which are vessels used solely for the purpose of pinpointing the best areas for drilling in the middle of oceans. It sounded like fun.

The owner–operator was experienced in commercial fishing and seemed to go about his business efficiently. He sourced the crew from the fishing industry and saved a packet, and for the fisherman this job would be a walk in the park compared to the hard, dangerous yakka of commercial fishing.

I flew to Singapore and waited in a hotel for nearly a month – on the payroll, so I wasn't complaining. Different people came and went, and everyone seemed to be having a good time. Eventually we went onboard, and promptly stepped off again – what a shit-box! Old, poorly equipped, run-down, filthy dirty and crawling with cockroaches. It was back to the hotel, just in time for happy hour.

The crew that had flown up from Australia had never been overseas before, and everything was an adventure. It didn't take them long to discover Singapore's seediest secrets, and for Singapore's seediest shysters to discover them.

The shitty little ship was fumigated and cleaned up a little. I looked scornfully at the orange-juice bottle with holes punched in it that was the shower nozzle, and tried to ignore the stench from the toilet, fermenting away in the hot, steamy Singapore climate. By this stage, the crew were knocked up with every STD imaginable, plus a few more that hadn't yet been classified, plus 'mechanical dandruff' – pubic lice.

I gave my cabin a scrub to try and make it habitable for the two- or three-week run down to Australia, but already the cockroaches were returning, as the eggs were hatching. One fumigation achieves fuck-all and it usually takes two or three goes to eradicate a ship infestation. But I'd come prepared with my silk sleeping-bag liner. The cockies can't get through the woven silk, so as long as you do it up tight they can only get your face. They do the most damage at night while you sleep as they eat the calluses off your heels, sometimes down to the raw flesh, which makes it very painful to walk around a moving deck.

I consoled myself with the US$1000 a day cash-in-hand, which included the month I'd been staying in the hotel, so I was well ahead.

Eventually, we sailed and made our way up Singapore Straits. It's a very busy place, and the high-density traffic requires a bit of concentration, but is no big deal when you've seen it many times before. Unfortunately, my crew had not, and they were terrified.

I stuck my head outside and was horrified to see an Australian flag flying proudly from the mast. I'd had the shipyard paint out the ship's name and port of registry as we were passing through waters in which pirates were known to operate. Now here we were, advertising to the world that we were Australians, loaded down with cash, Rolexes, and iPads.

'Who the fuck put that up?' I yelled.

'We did. We're Australians and we're proud of it,' came the reply.

I patiently explained the situation and the very real risk, but they weren't having it.

'If any pirate comes onboard we'll fix them up,' they said. 'Don't worry about that.'

Just the week before, two hours out of Singapore, pirates had boarded a large, modern bulk carrier and shot both the

Second Mate and the Master dead with bullets to the head. Here we were on a shitty little tug with a freeboard of about half a metre. Pirates could just step over the bulwark and saunter aboard, and our main form of defence was four piss-pot fishermen armed with a mop.

Down came the Aussie flag, and all the weather deck doors were locked down and padlocked from the inside. The only way in and out was via the wheelhouse doors, which was great for security, though not so great for fresh air. It was like a furnace inside.

I spent a lot of time in the wheelhouse where there was some respite, but more importantly I discovered that not one of my crew had the faintest idea about watchkeeping – keeping a proper lookout, collision avoidance, position fixing. They'd spent their whole lives staring at a GPS track plotter, and very rarely even seen a ship go past. Frankly, I was fucking terrified and barely slept a wink when off watch.

There were several very scary moments, but we somehow made our way clear of Singapore Straits and chugged off along the northern coastline of Sumatra and Java, towards Lombok Straits. Just as I was beginning to relax a little, all hell broke loose – one of the funnels was on fire!

A funnel fire becomes 'self- supporting' in that the exhaust blowing up the funnel keeps the fire roaring like a Roman candle, and you must move quickly as the heat is intense and the fire can easily spread. Thankfully, the fire extinguished itself when the starboard main engine was shut down, which was very lucky because I could see at a glance that no one onboard had the faintest idea what to do.

Then we discovered that not only was the cook absolutely shithouse, a classic fitter and turner (fit it into the oven and turn it into shit), but he had also come aboard with the flu, and it wasn't long before we all came down with it. Just what I needed on top of everything else.

We were still battened down with all the weather deck doors locked and bolted, and at night the decks were dark with only the navigation lights burning. One morning I came to the wheelhouse, leaned over the rail and found a little calling card.

'What's that on the railing?' I said to the lookout.

'Looks like a red rag,' he said.

'How did it get there?' I asked.

'Must have got washed up there when the bow's taken a wave?' he said.

'And tied in an overhand knot?'

Blank look.

'Let me explain it to you, mate. It's from night-time visitors. They come aboard at night and creep around in the dark seeing what there is to knock off. And when they leave, they leave a little calling card. Get the idea?'

News travelled fast and I could sense that all the rough, tough fishermen were pretty shaken by this, so I suggested they keep a sharper lookout, perhaps. In the next day or so we shaped up for the run down Lombok Strait and into the Indian Ocean, for the final run home to Dampier. I was on watch around 10pm, at the chart table, when I noticed a long, dark open boat manoeuvring alongside on our starboard side. I leaped for the autopilot tiller and pushed it hard to starboard, then ran right over the fucker. There was a bang and a thud; I put the rudders hard to port and brought her back on track. I pushed the general alarm, and at the same time gave an 'all stations' call over VHF-16 that there may be a boat requiring assistance. Don't know, don't care.

Within minutes, the little wheelhouse was full, everyone jabbering nervously.

'Get yourselves into two-man teams and check the ship, especially the engine room. I don't know whether the boat was just coming alongside, or whether it's been alongside and was just departing. Either way, check around and make sure there's no one onboard.'

Well, so much for the tough guys. Nobody fucking moved. Eventually two of them left the wheelhouse carrying a large fire axe – handy thing to try and swing in a confined engine room, I thought. Nothing; no one onboard, much to everyone's obvious relief.

'What about the boat?' someone asked.

'Fuck the boat,' everyone else said in unison, and it seemed that some of them at least were learning.

After midnight we were heading down into Lombok Strait, which has some ferocious tidal flows as the South China Sea flows into the Indian Ocean. On some voyages, I've had five knots of current on the nose. As the outgoing southerly tidal stream meets head-on with the heavy northerly weather in the Indian Ocean, it sometimes makes for a very confused sea.

Sometimes, the collision of the two makes a 'hole' in the sea, which is not so noticeable on a large ship; however, on a smaller ship, it can be quite dramatic. It certainly was this time, as the little ship dove headfirst into a hole like a diving submarine. Then it hit a solid wall of water at the bottom and stopped dead. Everything that wasn't secured kept going forward, which included the navigational/communications PC, all the books and loose equipment, and anyone not hanging on. As she crawled out of the hole and reached for the sky, the port main engine lost oil pressure and shut itself down. The bow fell away downwind, and we were now heading for the steep cliffs, and at a good pace. With only one propeller she could not bring her head to weather, so it was necessary to take a round turn out of her, which brought the cliffs even closer. Fortunately there was a bit of moon, so it was easy to see the shoreline – all of the GPS systems had gone offline, so it was back to basics. Eventually we clawed our way out of the confused sea and into stable water. The port main engine was restarted and everything settled down.

It was quite a day for the boys!

We waddled our way south across the Indian Ocean, thankfully avoiding any cyclones, and with great relief entered the Port of Dampier. The owner was waiting on the wharf, and, after I got my money, I told him where he could stick his fucking job! I doubt the boys would be jumping at another such travel adventure anytime soon.

ALF

I was always very keen on flying and even took flying lessons at 16. I used to ride my bike 10 kilometres to the Royal Victorian Aero Club at Moorabbin Airport. I was very keen, but went to sea instead of pursuing flying.

I got my private pilot's licence 50 years ago, accumulating 2500 hours with endorsements for twin-engine, night visual flight rules (VFR), retractable gear and constant speed prop. A lot of my seafaring skills stood me in good stead in the air: knowing how to use a radio properly and keeping a good lookout, along with understanding rules, regulations and disciplines. I still get a thrill lifting from the runway, looking down at the earth from high in the sky and cloud-dancing (illegally).

For one licence test, I was required to fly with a CASA inspector instead of the usual instructor. I waited around the tarmac and he eventually showed up, running late.

'What time are we meant to get away?' he asked.

'O-six-hundred,' I replied, which was accepted practice on ships.

He looked at me like I was an insect.

'I'll come back another day,' he said, 'when you learn to tell the time properly. O is a letter not a number.'

It was a very exciting day when I bought my first aircraft VH-CGT ('Charlie, Golf, Tango'): a second-hand, ex-flying school Piper Warrior II. I remember sitting on the fence and just looking at it in awe. As a family, thanks to flying, we travelled up and down the East Coast of Australia, made some lifelong friends, and had some scares – but many more great times and adventures.

One afternoon I visited a friend of a friend who had his own bush strip and hangar on his property. Tucked away inside the hangar, under a linen dust-cover, was an immaculate Cessna 172. C172s are like Holden Commodores: most are pretty basic and have had a hard life. But this one, VH-AKZ, was 'as new', with a sharp paint job and every conceivable extra. He'd bought it at the Oshkosh Airshow in the USA from a Delta Airlines captain, and it was the best presented and equipped C172 in Australia. For me, it was love at first sight. A year later it came up for sale, our mutual friend brokered and VH-AKZ ('Alpha, Kilo, Zulu') became mine.

There was a cardboard box full of instruction manuals and other stuff that hadn't been sent with the plane, but I couldn't get hold of the owner and was getting a bit pissed off. I called our mutual friend, explained my frustration, and asked him if he knew where the owner was.

'I know exactly where he is,' came the reply, 'he's right in front of me.'

'Well, put him on the fucking phone,' I said.

'Not possible. You see, he's right in front of me, in a coffin, in the back of a hearse, and we're on the way to his funeral.' WTF! Well, I'd just have to work out the instructions on my own.

One afternoon with some rare free time from reef piloting, I took 'Alf' out for a flight from Mackay, which has a lovely long runway for commercial jet aircraft that heads out into sea, and I was familiar with the airport requirements and clearances.

After taxiing out and getting the final clearances, I eased the power up, plucked Alf off the runway, and started to climb out at full power while still tracking overhead the remaining runway. Just as I was nearing the airport perimeter, the engine started to miss and play up, which, let's just say, came as something of a shock. I did my checks quickly and thoroughly but to no avail; with a final splutter the engine stopped and so did the propeller. Just silence. WTF?!

Now was definitely the time to worry, but I didn't have a lot of time as the ground was coming up fast. I could still see the end of the active runway, and the temptation to turn and descend was incredibly hard to resist. But it had been drilled into me time and time again: you'll never make it – ever.

Ahead of me was the bright-blue sea and a few sandbars close to the shore, so I got the nose down to keep some airspeed, picked a spot on the sandbar and locked onto it. I did my final forced-landing checks, called 'Mayday' and opened the door so it wouldn't jam on impact. I pulled my harness and belts tight, and braced.

Mackay Tower left me alone after acknowledging my Mayday, and I focused on flaring Alf out and stalling him onto the sandbar at a slow speed. That was the plan anyway. As the wheels touched the wet sand, Alf bounced and leaped into the air again, as if he had one last chance to avoid his fate. But Alf lost airspeed with the bounce and came to earth with a crash – except it wasn't earth at this stage, it was the sea.

It didn't take long for the cabin to fill and it was a nervy few minutes before I could force the door open against the water pressure, pop the harness, ditch the headset and drag myself out the door. It was easy to get to the sandbar and start the long wade back to shore; I could already see two police officers coming out towards me, and the airport rescue fire truck arriving on the beach.

A crowd had gathered on the beach by the time I made it back, and somebody knew somebody who was on his way with a big sugarcane-farm tractor and a long rope. The tide was due to flood, so the window of opportunity to recover Alf was getting smaller by the minute.

One of the aircraft mechanics had turned up, and when he heard what was going on, he pulled me aside and cautioned me not to touch it until I had approval from the insurance company, otherwise any damage I did from here wouldn't be covered. I found a phone and eventually got hold of an insurance rep in Melbourne, and frantically explained what was happening, but they fucked around and approval never came. The tide did, though, and Alf floated out to sea.

By the time I got back to the airport office, I was pretty upset because I knew I could have recovered the aircraft. I called my wife to let her know I was okay, and to make sure that the insurance was up to date.

'I haven't got time for this,' she said. 'I'm just taking the cat to the vet because it's got an anal problem.' *Click.* I'd always had a suspicion that my position on the family totem pole was fairly low down – but I didn't think that I was even lower than a cat's arsehole.

The CASA air crash investigator, an experienced flying instructor, questioned me about the incident. He was in no doubt that I would never have made it if I had tried to get back down onto the end of the runway. I would have ended up as a burnt patch of blackened grass, he said, and in the obituary column of the *Mackay Bugle*.

Alf washed up on another beach three days later, totally wrecked, and ended up being parted out for scrap. It was a very sad end, but the cat's bum was fine.

DRUNKEN PARROTS

Sugar is big business in Queensland, and Mackay is a major sugar exporting port (800,000 tonnes of raw sugar per year). The sugar-loading wharf is kept busy with at least one Panamax a week (a Panamax is a ship designed and built to just squeeze through the Panama Canal). After the bulk carrier has departed, there are frequently patches of sugar left, sometimes for days. The local lorikeets have learned to make the most of it, and flocks of them arrive to party!

As all good sailors know, sugar together with (rain) water, and a bit of tropical heat ferments into alcohol, and the lorikeets lap it up: colourful T-shirts, shouting, yelling, telling stories; getting loud, friendly, excited, pushing and shoving; the fighting starts, and after a while they quieten down. Some look a bit unhappy, some look sick, and some of them fall over, unconscious, with their feet in the air and wings outstretched. It takes a few hours, and then they're ready to go again. It all seems vaguely familiar?!

THE BODY IN THE CARGO OFFICE

Our handsome pilot launch came alongside the scruffy ship with a gentle thud. I was joining this ship to bring it through Trinity Passage, inside the Barrier Reef and up to Cape Flattery for a load of silica sand.

There was a manky pilot ladder hanging down, as well as a dodgy-looking heaving line for my bag. The deckie helped me onto the foot of the pilot ladder and I started the long clamber up the rusty ship's side. To my left, I could see the old heaving line hauling my bag up when, suddenly, *bang!* It parted and my bag crashed to the foredeck of the pilot boat, burst open, and everything went in the drink. WTF.

The deckie moved quickly and, together with the coxswain, retrieved most of my belongings and sent them up in a black garbage bag (known in the trade as an 'offshore Samsonite').

Meanwhile, halfway up the side of the ship, I was shitting myself because the rope ladder I was on looked in a very similar condition to the heaving line that had just carried away. When I clambered over the bulwark and was safely on deck, fright gave way to fury and I tore the Filipino deck crew another arsehole, collectively. I was in a foul mood.

Entering into the accommodation via the weather deck watertight door and taking a deep breath before climbing the ten flights of stairs to the bridge, I passed by the open doorway of the deck cargo office, which was strewn with old papers, rags and flattened cardboard boxes.

On top of this mess was a dead body – still in overalls, but with the broken leg bone poking through the orange material. The body was curled up, but it was easy to see that the side of his skull was flattened by an impact or fall.

It was a big shock, and one of the crew told me he'd just died; he'd fallen down a cargo hold (20 metres) and died. *Probably on one of those fucking ropes,* I thought. As I was taking in this scene, I saw the man's eyes flicker, and then noticed his chest rise and fall – he was breathing!

'He's not dead,' I said.

'Well, he's nearly dead,' came the reply.

I got to the bridge as quickly as I could, charged up to the big fat Filipino captain and yelled, 'Your crew member is not dead, he is still alive!'

'No, he is nearly dead,' said the captain, and that was that.

I piloted the ship through the narrow passage in the reef, into the safe waters of the inner reef and then got on my cell phone to the rescue helicopter service. I knew them well; their hangar was next to ours for our pilot transfer helicopter. The captain interrupted - he was furious, babbling away about who was going to pay for helicopters and medical attention. The more I ignored him, the angrier he got - he was going right off.

The rescue helicopter launched straight away and within minutes was onboard. Two paramedics ran up the deck with their bags and equipment, while the captain crept off to his bridge chair, glowering. I expected the medics to come out quickly with the injured man on their stretcher, but nothing happened for a long time. Then the helicopter powered down and the rotors stopped turning, which was very unusual.

As the ship was now safe and on course, I left the bridge and the sulking fat captain and raced down the stairs to the weather deck office. It was like a scene from a hospital emergency TV show. The place was littered with tear-offs from the medics' equipment, and they were going hard. One looked up and recognised me.

'We only just managed to get him going again - only just,' he said.

The injured man was eventually stabilised enough for the helicopter transfer to hospital, and we endured a very quiet trip up to Cape Flattery.

I found out later that the man had compound fractures to both legs, multiple internal injuries and his skull had been compressed flat on one side. But he survived. Myself and another reef pilot took him some magazines and stuff but he wasn't too well at the time, and didn't know who we were. I have never understood the ship's crew members' reaction. Surely he must have had some friends amongst the crew? Someone who would care enough to give some sort of basic first aid, lay him down, put a pillow under his head, try to make him comfortable and clean him up a bit? No. They just threw him in the filthy office like a discarded doll and left him to die a slow, lonely and painful death. I don't get it.

JOINING SEA SHEPHERD

Sea Shepherd have always been a controversial group, and while I'm not a tree-hugger, I do believe in some of the causes they fight so very hard for. Top of the list for me would be the unnecessary slaughter of whales by the Japanese in the name of 'research', in our territorial waters. Because of that, I am just one of the many volunteer crew members who have given their time to Sea Shepherd.

I did not agree with all of Sea Shepherd's goals, and over the ten years I worked with them I only went on the campaigns that interested me, which Sea Shepherd management always respected and never questioned. I enjoyed every day on those campaigns and was always treated well onboard their ships, all of which are maintained to a high standard and kept clean and tidy. I enjoy ship-handling – hands-on 'driving' ships – and it's a demanding skill given the variety of ships, propulsion and control systems, and weather (usually bad) that you might encounter. Some of the most demanding driving I've ever done has been on these ships.

But I do have one insurmountable problem, which is that the galleys are entirely vegetarian – and I'm not! Vegetarianism sits well with the principles of Sea Shepherd, but it's also an important requirement because all foodstuffs are donated. It's easier and safer to maintain the quality and cleanliness of donated vegetable products than donated fish, meats and poultry, which easily spoil.

Most of the time it was no big deal, since the vegetarian dishes served varied widely and the freshly baked breads were always sensational, but after a few weeks I'd had enough; I needed meat! While up inside the Arctic Circle on the *Steve Irwin* at anchor, with the sun still in the sky at 10pm, I took a walk around the decks. As I got up to the helideck there was the unmistakeable, mouth-watering aroma of freshly cooked bacon. I 'bird-dogged' it down to the small maintenance workshop inside the dark hangar to find both the helicopter pilot and engineer crouched over a small George Foreman grill, turning over the bacon rashers with a pair of long-nosed pliers. Their little battery headlights showed their looks of terror at being sprung – quite a surprise considering they were both US Marine Corps combat veterans!

So, I joined the secret club, with membership gained by covertly purchasing a pack of bacon rashers when next in port. It was hardly a secret because everyone onboard guessed what was happening as we disappeared out the door with a big serve of vegetarian lasagne – to be mixed later with crispy bacon! Yum!

My shipmates back onboard were always a very mixed bunch. Every nationality imaginable, generally 50/50 male/female, every age group, and every type of background – except, for the most part, seafaring! There were welders, carpenters, ditch-diggers, truckies, firefighters, servicemen and women, hairdressers, ice-cream salespeople, hardcore patched bikies, priests, monks, salespeople, lawyers, posties, real estate agents and world travellers. There was never a dull moment at mealtimes, but all were dedicated and enthusiastic. You had to be dedicated to buy your own airfare halfway around the world to a place you'd never heard of then spend five weeks swinging a mop.

The ships always had a very confident Bosun and an AB to get things moving, and within a week they had the crew performing tasks they'd never dreamed of doing: launching and recovering the big powerful RIBs (rigid inflatable boats) in all weathers and both day and night, helping launch and recover the helicopter and amphibious ultra-light, working in the engine room and galley, mopping decks and companionways and standing bridge watches.

Occasionally, very occasionally, there was an arsehole.

I came across one on the bridge while heading across from Aberdeen. She came from a very well-to-do British family and didn't quite understand how a ship functions – in particular, the level of authority that any ship's Master has. She was obviously very used to getting her own way, and as

Daddy had made a considerable donation, she felt that she was entitled to run the show.

Big mistake.

That night, she got fed up with the boredom of a long sea watch and decided to go down and turn in, leaving the nightwatch on the bridge one lookout down – not acceptable. She was called back and I explained to her that she had signed on to stand a watch, and she wasn't to leave the bridge until relieved by the oncoming watch. This didn't suit her, and she threw a pretty impressive tantrum threatening me with all sorts of pain. After 15 minutes of this I'd had enough. I told her to get off my bridge and go below. She refused, so I had the Bosun and a couple of hands attend the bridge and remove her. I was well within my rights (as I very well knew), and I was fully supported by management. She was put ashore at the next port. Bye!

A ship is a ship, and has to be managed correctly if it's to function safely, smoothly, efficiently and harmoniously – no exceptions.

My presence onboard as an experienced Master was always welcomed as all were hungry for the knowledge and experience I could offer. During some dead days in the Shetlands, I ran some short lectures on celestial navigation and the messroom was packed. I spent ten years teaching Master 4 part-time, so it was not hard for me to do, and it was a lot of fun. I enjoyed teasing them just as I did my Master 4 students. I'd point out to them that all of the planets had moons, some more than one, and I'd rattle off a few of their names: Mars has two and one is named Phobos, Jupiter has a lot and one is Ganymede, Saturn has heaps and one is called Titan. Then I'd mention that our earth only has one – what's its name?

There was always a thunderous silence until someone would sheepishly say, '... Moon?' Everyone would look awkward until the proper name was finally offered: 'Luna'.

On some occasions I could easily fix a problem with which the rest of the crew were mightily stuck, usually because they were too kind and caring – attributes not common amongst professional Masters. A good example was when I discovered we had a grub in the galley. With 45 people onboard and meals 24 hours a day, it was essential that a high standard of cleanliness was observed – that included personal cleanliness, too. A scruffy-looking woman had joined, having spent the previous three years backpacking around India and living rough. She could prepare some interesting dishes, but she was so dirty she was crawling – quite literally, with little black insects living in her dreadlocks, dirty black fingernails, filthy clothes and sandals, and she stank like a dunny door on a prawn trawler. But no one would make the call; no one knew what to do, nor did they want the unpleasant task of doing something about it!

I had just joined the ship, and the instant I heard about the problem, I leaped out of my bridge chair and took off down the stairs to the galley.

It was pretty easy to sniff out the culprit. WTF.

There is no place in any galley for dirty people – ever, no exceptions.

'You, out!' I said firmly. 'And don't return to the galley. Get cleaned up, wash your clothes and see the Bosun, who will find a job for you elsewhere. If that doesn't suit you, then the Bosun will show you the gangway on arrival.'

Problem solved. I could see upon my returning to the wheelhouse that it was a great relief to all.

There were always a few fuck-ups, which was not a surprise given the duties were mostly imposed upon people who'd never ever seen a ship let alone been to sea.

The long-suffering Bosun had seen it all. He was a very experienced and capable bloke who was also a drummer in a heavy metal band (he had a drum kit set up in the foc'sle store, and I really enjoyed listening to him practice!). He was a wild-looking guy, and when he spoke, everyone listened. How he had the patience to address a continuously changing crowd of blank faces never ceased to amaze me.

Launching and recovering a boat while underway (moving through the water) is a difficult task even for full-time professional sailors, and quite daunting for a bunch of hairdressers, chemists, North American Indian chiefs and long-haul locomotive drivers. The Bosun couldn't be everywhere at once, and a moment's distraction could be disastrous, as proved to be the case.

As we left a port one day, the Bosun came to see me on the bridge to ask if it was okay to run one more boat-launching practice, as he felt the new launch crew were finally getting somewhere. He didn't want to put the boat in the water for this practice, just float it off its cradle, swing it out over the starboard side with the HIAB crane, run the painter (the boat's long bow line) and trice it into the ship's side to allow the boat crew to safely board.

'No problem,' I said.

As we had come onto our course line and the engines were set (two Ruston-Paxman diesels of 4380 hp coupled to one shaft/propeller), I handed over the bridge watch and went down to my cabin. It had been a long day and I was looking forward to putting my feet up.

The Master's cabin is always on the starboard side and forward-looking (for obvious reasons). As I stepped inside, I heard the unmistakable scream of a winch wire being stripped off its drum. I looked out of my porthole just in time to see the 5-tonne HIAB crane be ripped from its pedestal and crash onto the deck like a dead animal, the deck awash with panicked people!

I raced back to the bridge, and from the wing I could see instantly what had happened. I put the rudder to starboard to cant the stern and propeller away from anyone in the water, then pulled the pitch to zero to take the way off.

The inexperienced deck crew had not followed the

Bosun's instructions when releasing the brake, and the big RIB had been accidentally lowered down to the water, now rushing past at 14 knots. The painter (the boat's bow line) had not been properly secured and the boat instantly filled up like a bucket. The huge load put upon the crane wire sheered the crane's base bolts, and it fell onto the deck and bulwark. All the people in the boat had been washed overboard in the mighty surge and were now bobbing about in our wake.

As our way came off, the Bosun was able to haul the RIB back up the ship's side with a winch, but we couldn't quickly launch any of our other boats as our crane was now deceased. I could now move our ship astern and get close enough to put our gangway down and into the water. The men and women in the water swam across, oblivious to the danger, and I had to hit the emergency stops and shut the main engines down before they were sucked into the blender. The massive propeller might be in zero pitch with no thrust, but it was still spinning at full RPM.

Luck was on our side and all hands were recovered with nothing worse than a good dunking. During the night, our deck crew and engineers recovered the boat to its cradle and reset the crane on its base. Everything was back to normal – but we'd dodged a bullet, that's for sure!

My time spent driving these ships was a pleasure, but challenging.

A partially trained chimpanzee could take a ship from A to B with a professional staff of officers, engineers and seamen, and the very latest in navigational equipment. But it's a bit more involved when the ship is old and not so generously equipped and you have to rely on very willing yet totally inexperienced people to achieve the same outcome. It requires a great deal of self-control not to lose it when things go wrong, and also to lavish praise when even the most simple of tasks is completed.

But when you walk down the gangway for the last time and the whole crew turn out to bid you farewell – it's very satisfying, and very humbling.

GREAT DANES

Even after 50 years at sea, my time with Sea Shepherd had plenty of surprises. At one point my ship was arrested and a writ stuck on the mast by Lord Mackay of Drummadore's Master at arms – a new experience for me! I spent a bit of time alongside in Lerwick in the Shetland Islands until, one million US dollars later, we were free to go.

Steaming up and down the spectacular fjords of the (Norwegian) Faroe Islands was also an adventure, as was getting into some of the tiny ports tucked away there. Our donated charts were not reliable, and the harbour entrances were sometimes not much wider than the ship. I was glad of the skills I'd developed as a Torres Strait and Great Barrier Reef marine pilot, taking ships up and down the Reef. It was quite a challenge to get a volunteer (a welder from Estonia, in this case) up to speed with helm orders, which then freed me up to 'con' the ship using voice commands.

Needless to say we weren't always popular wherever we went. In Tórshavn, the main port of the Faroes, no sooner had we tied up and shut down than the local coppers trooped aboard to remind us of the local laws. A couple of dirty, big coppers, fully rigged, came to the wheelhouse along with a super good-looking female cop with a long blonde ponytail who asked me to accompany her to the local police HQ. No problem!

I was treated well and put in an interview room where a succession of increasingly senior police officers came in to tell me pretty much the same thing: break the law, and you'll be arrested. Each successively higher-ranking copper got bigger in size, until the last one, a true giant, had to stoop down to get under the door frame. I was impressed; as a demonstration of strength and power, it worked on me!

This last gigantic copper bid me farewell and told me to wait – apparently now the chief superintendent, the el supremo, had decided to see me as well. I gazed at the doorframe trying to guess what size this final monster might be, when in darted a tiny older lady dressed in a trim suit and pearls. She may have been small – very small – but she spoke with authority.

I was caught totally off-guard after the procession of giants, and told her so. She had a good laugh and we chatted for a bit, mainly about Australia and how much she would like to visit Down Under. She saw me to the door and wished me well, but I was left in no doubt that justice would be swift and sure if we stuck our nose where not invited!

ABOARD THE
BRIGITTE BARDOT

When I completed my 'swing' onboard *Steve Irwin*, I headed back to Aberdeen on the high-speed trimaran *Brigitte Bardot*, which would take about 24 hours to cover the 380 miles at an economical speed. She was originally built to break the around-the-world speed record, which she did in 75 days back in 1998. Sleek and fast, built of exotic composite materials and powered by two 500 hp Cummins diesels, she was pretty impressive at 35 metres long and 41 tonnes.

When I stepped aboard I was met by one of the Discovery Channel's *Whale Wars* team: a slightly built woman with a massive camera on her shoulder. She asked if I was prone to seasickness. (I was, on occasions, but I wasn't going to admit that to her!)

'If you don't get seasick, I guarantee you will on here,' she said, and offered me a few scop transdermal patches but I declined. These patches release a drug (scopolamine) through the skin to counter seasickness, and they work very well, but the side effects could stun a bull. As the woman turned and walked away, I could see that she had two stuck on her neck – twice the recommended dosage!

It was pretty crammed inside the ship but nice and warm, which would be a benefit while crossing the North Atlantic Ocean – or so I thought …

Once we cleared the Faroes the weather worsened, and before long we were in a full-blown North Atlantic gale. I very quickly discovered that trimarans, at reduced power and in a heavy seaway, were a perfect recipe for seasickness. OMG! Give me that scop patch, please! There is only one known and proven cure for seasickness – that is, to sit under a tree. And that wasn't an option right now!

We flogged away into the night and the weather worsened, and at around midnight the noise changed as the starboard main engine shat itself.

The engineer, a great bloke from Belgium whose hobby and business was rebuilding ex-Soviet Kamov military helicopters, lifted the plates and slid in on his back under the mighty (but now very quiet) Cummins. The engine space was very confined, the two main engines staggered so as to fit inside the very narrow hull.

Within minutes, we realised the engineer was in great difficulty. Seasickness had hit him, not surprisingly, but he couldn't fully turn his head in the confined space and was choking on his own vomit. We dragged him out by his feet and cleaned him up as best we could. Unfortunately the smell of fresh spew is always a catalyst for a chain reaction, which now included me!

The previously warm and cosy cabin became very stuffy and smelly, and there was no chance to even open a door in the wild weather. The little ship pitched, rolled, heaved and yawed all at the same time, and the various creaks and groans as the hulls flexed didn't inspire me with great confidence.

We pushed on through the night and it was around noon that we finally limped into Aberdeen Harbour and made fast to the stone quay. I crawled across the deck and off the ship, then rolled onto my back on the dirty cobblestones – thank fuck that was over. Never again.

It was time to find a pub. Aberdeen is a very busy base for the North Sea Oilfields, and I could see a few offshore 'anchor clankers' were alongside. Sure enough, small groups of seamen were coming off the ships and meeting up together on the wharf, then making a beeline for a pub. I galloped off down the road with my bag.

Within the space of a couple of beers, my 'credentials' had been tested and approved, and I was an accepted part of the team. A worldwide language of sailorman really does exist!

LOCAL PUBLICAN

Over the years of owning a hobby farm in country Victoria, where my wife and I raised our kids, I've got friendly with the local farrier. One afternoon, while attending our horses and ponies, he mentioned that the local country pub was under new management and was well worth a visit.

We decided to round up the wives and meet for lunch there the next day.

Walking through the public bar and into the lounge, it didn't look like too much had changed: there was a new publican there alright, but he didn't give us much of a welcome – in fact, I thought it was more of a dirty look. We sat down, and he lifted the flap and marched straight for us. I sensed that there was some history between us, and a new chapter was about to be written.

'I remember you,' he said. 'You were Master on the XXX, and you sacked me!'

Here's a problem, I thought.

'I was sacked for drinking, and because it was my third offence, I was finished up. Never allowed to go to sea again,' he said, in a way that was so calm that it was chilling. 'I had a young family and found myself on the beach with no job. It hit me very hard.'

The wives were looking around them nervously when this memory emerged. It had been 20 years earlier and an all-too-familiar occurrence in those days. An abundance of cheap grog, strong personalities and a cavalier attitude to life was a recipe for disaster for some seamen.

As a ship's Master it was important to fix problems efficiently, and to strike hard and decisively, otherwise the 'crowd' would walk over you. This guy was pissed on the job, so in the logbook he went and down the gangway shortly afterwards, never to be seen again. Until this moment 20 years later.

I was on guard and ready to duck. My big, tough farrier mate had somehow slipped away, and it was just me and the publican pretty much standing toe to toe.

'It was the best thing that ever happened to me,' he said. 'I was a drunk and a no-hoper, and that was a big turning point in my life. I never drank again and got a job as a barman just to prove a point.' He'd progressed through all levels of management with a big company and was now employed as a 'fix-it' manager, moving from pub to pub. 'You helped make me what I am today,' he said, 'so choose a nice bottle of wine, on my account, and please enjoy your lunch.'

PALLIATIVE POWER

My younger sister was losing the fight of her life and was in palliative care. We had never been very close, but this was the end of the line and it was with a heavy heart I jumped on my motorcycle and headed down to see her.

I pulled into the hospital car park, and made my way to the entrance in my leathers, with my helmet and gloves in hand.

'G'day,' said a guy waiting just inside the door. He looked tidy despite his shorts, T-shirt and thongs, and had lots of tubes and stuff hanging out of his arm. 'I saw the 'Busa come in,' he said, 'a '99, too. It looks awesome.'

He was referring to my 1999 Hayabusa, the fastest road bike ever made (we're talking upwards of 300 kph). It was indeed awesome, but this was an intensely awkward moment because I was in no mood for chit-chat, and I guessed this guy was on the same one-way trip as my sister.

'Should have stayed on my bike,' he went on, 'and the cigarettes and grog, too – doesn't make much difference now, really!'

I scuttled off, not really knowing how to answer. I spent time with my sister and her family and friends, and then it was time to go. I made eye contact with my sister as I backed out the door, and we both knew it was a final goodbye. I can still see the moment now. Life is so very fucking cruel.

At the exit, the bloke in the shorts was still hanging around and gave me a little wave, but I didn't feel like talking, even about motorbikes. I headed straight to the car park, put my balaclava, gloves and helmet on, and jumped aboard. I fired up the big 'Busa and noticed the guy was at the window watching, and I felt awful for not engaging him more.

I rode slowly up the garden path to the hospital door, and the bloke came out like a rocket.

'Thought ya might like a closer look, mate?' I said.

He did a couple of circles around my bike, making all the right noises. He knew his stuff.

'Jump on,' I said.

'Now?'

'Course. What have you got to lose?'

So he kicked his thongs off and jumped on the back

'Helmet?' he asked.

'Who fucking cares, eh?'

I worked my way out of the car park, onto the highway, and let her go. He was hanging onto my jacket, laughing so hard he nearly fell off, his tubes and things blowing in the wind.

I went for a couple of clicks, very, very fast, and then I dropped him off at the door again.

He had tears streaming down his face – from the wind, but also from his heart.

He gave me a hug and put his thongs back on, just as a very angry nurse burst out the door.

'What on earth are you doing?!' she yelled. 'This man is very sick and you've got him on a bike with no protective gear. He could have been killed!'

'Yeah, that's a big fucking worry for him,' I said. We laughed. I gave the guy a slap on the shoulder and a big wink, and for the second time that day, I made eye contact that will be with me forever. Then I was gone.

I heard nothing more about the guy but I know I made him cry with delight at what must have been the most awful time in his life. I hope somebody would do it for me.

SWALLOWING THE ANCHOR

This expression is very old sailor talk. When a seafarer has had enough and wants to finally settle ashore, never to return to sea, he's 'swallowed the anchor'. Frequently, seafarers who swallow the anchor and move ashore like to get as far away from the sea as possible; the sea holds no further attraction for them, and possibly never did in the first place. The work and the ships and the camaraderie are the attraction, not staring at the endless sea.

I never wanted to live near the sea, but loved the idea of having a parcel of land in the country. My wife and I kept searching further and further out until we found something in 1980 that matched our miserable funds. We loved it immediately.

It was a wild bush block of 20 acres in a very remote area complete with birds and animals and flies – lots of flies. We hacked away at it, and within a few years had a comfortable house, a shed and stable, and a perimeter fence.

We had no immediate neighbours back then. The closest house was a tumbledown derelict, although you could see it had been a considerable pile in its day, complete with extensive gardens and a fine tree that seemed to revel in the neglect. When a family moved in and tidied everything up, it was easy to see that it was quite a beauty, and one afternoon while having a yabber it came out that the property had originally been owned and established by a ship's captain – Captain Trevor, whom our little road had been named after!

It was incredible to think that I had followed the footsteps of another captain, nearly a century later, to this small dead-end road in a very remote area. We have lived in this house for over 40 years, and I never want to live anywhere else. The best thing about it is there's not a ship in sight.

Now that I'm 'on the beach' pretty much for good, I'm frequently asked, do I miss the sea?

No.

I do miss some things such as the ships and the people, the challenges and the excitement of a good fuck-up, but not the sea itself. Only weekend sailors and mudskippers use terms such as 'the sea in my blood', 'my first love is the sea', or 'a natural-born salty sailorman'. True 'blue-water' seafarers never use such words because they don't need to. Perhaps more importantly they never speak lightly or frivolously about something they know can kill them in an instant, or smash their world apart.

I also don't miss the loneliness. Being the Master of a ship is mostly a lonely existence, by necessity. The Master must be absolutely responsible for everything, and friendships can impede the functioning of this system.

But there is something I *really* miss, which is hard to duplicate ashore, and that is being able to stand alone on a bridge wing and gaze at the endless sea and the deep depth of the stars, and be made aware of just how totally insignificant we really are.

When you finally leave a ship, whether the journey was good, bad, or ghastly, and you trudge along the wharf with your suitcase, you always stop, pause and look back and say to yourself, 'That wasn't so bad'.

That's what I'm doing right now.

THANKS

Writing this has been a big adventure for me, a steep learning curve and a hatful of surprises. The amazing process of transforming a memory stick full of random words into a book has been the job of the hard-working, oppressed and grossly underpaid 'crew' at Affirm Press, under the tyrannical command of Martin Hughes, 'Master under God'. They were always polite and patient, even when breaking the news to me that the use of four exclamation marks in one sentence is (apparently) unacceptable. However, in return, they also learned a few things from me, including that a well-placed profanity is a powerful fucking tool!

The starting point for this book, the kick in the pants, came many years ago from two separate sources: Alison Lester and Chris Roering, both accomplished wordsmiths and long-term friends (and still unknown to each other!). I am very grateful for their unwavering faith.

There are many, many more who have helped me, including the ship-loads of seafarers who have unwittingly and unwillingly become part of my story. Please accept my apologies, or contact my lawyer.

And a big thanks to the deep blue sea – it pays us and then it claims us.